PEARSON **LITERATURE**

*NATIONAL*

# All-in-One
# Workbook
# Answer Key

*The American Experience*

## PEARSON

Upper Saddle River, New Jersey
Boston, Massachusetts
Chandler, Arizona
Glenview, Illinois
Shoreview, Minnesota

13-digit ISBN: 978-0-13-366820-9
10-digit ISBN: 0-13-366820-7

1 2 3 4 5 6 7 8 9 10    12 11 10 09 08

# ANSWERS

## Unit 1

### Names and Terms to Know Worksheet, p. 1

**A (Possible answers)**

1. first British colony in America
2. British law that charged a tax on American colonists
3. belief in hard work and self-discipline
4. colonist from Africa who wrote about his experiences
5. author of the Declaration of Independence, third president
6. French farmer who settled in New York and wrote "Letters"

**B (Possible responses)**

1. Religious persecution led the Puritans to leave Europe and settle in the New World. They hoped that their new surroundings would provide a setting to create a perfected society.
2. New England settlers came in search of religious freedom; southern colonists in search of opportunity. The climate of New England was harsher than that of the South; the southern economy depended on cotton, which in turn depended on slaves.
3. The Founding Fathers valued Enlightenment reason and logic and were familiar with the "social contract" described by John Locke, in which people consent to be governed.

### Essential Question Worksheet, p. 2

**A. (Possible responses)**

1. a. magnificent and challenging
   b. that people were part of nature, and did not own it
2. a. to mankind
   b. setting for a perfect society
   c. harsh and dangerous
   d. one of great security and self-reliance
3. a. turn a savage land into a godly one
   b. more manageable and less threatening

**B. (Possible responses)**

1. untamed and unsettled
2. the Sierra Nevada Mountains
3. poisonous snakes

### Essential Question Worksheet p. 3

**A. (Possible answers)**

1. a. the lesson or insight about life conveyed by a literary work
   b. the plot, characters, setting, images, symbols, and comments of the author
2. a. admiration for its magnificence
   b. community and indepdence
   c. self-reliance and individualism
3. a. uniqueness, terror, beauty

   b. Many European traditions were of no use to them.
   c. a new and unique people

**B. (Possible responses)**

1. agree to accept another's directions
2. that he would overcome them
3. we had to prepare for the big assembly

### Essential Question Worksheet, p. 4

**A. (Possible answers)**

1. a. their religious beliefs
   b. logic, reason, clear thinking
   c. Native Americans and African slaves
2. a. Native American oral poets, de Cardenas, Cabeza de Vaca, William Bradford
   b. Cotton Mather, Thomas Paine, Thomas Jefferson
   c. Olaudah Equiano, Benjamin Franklin

**B. (Possible responses_**

1. was able to lead others
2. celebrating special holidays
3. good works

### Follow-Through Activities, p. 5

**A Check Your Comprehension**

Guidelines: Students should complete the chart with other concepts appropriate to the period and the groups that are associated with these concepts.

**B. Extend Your Learning**

Guidelines: Students should complete the chart with answers that will help them to research a form of spoken literature from the early period of American history.

### From the Author's Desk

### Susan Power Introduces "Museum Indians," p. 6

1. The term *oral tradition* refers to the repetition of stories within a community, in which they are passed down from one generation to the next and thus kept alive. Spoken stories are performed before a live audience of all ages.
2. She means that each retelling of a story changes it a little; the stories are modified according to the choices made by individual storytellers, as well as by any given audience's mood and tastes.
3. She was very shy as a child and silent in her classes, finding it difficult to stand before an audience and present a story or an idea.
4. She was fascinated by the rhythmic poetry of the language. She thinks that Shakespeare would have been attracted to the dramatic aspects of Native American oral literature.
5. She means that she did not encounter much bicultural literature, or stories about people growing up in two worlds at once.

6. Contrasts may include the following: begins earlier in time vs. begins later in time; requires language but not a writing system vs. requires both language and a writing system; based on memory and oral transmission vs. based on texts that can be written down, read, and copied; includes folklore, proverbs, chants, and ballads vs. includes novels, short stories, history books; uses strong rhythms and repetition to help memory vs. uses less repetition because memory is not essential; performer can vary presentation in response to audience vs. writer cannot vary text; material can change with each presentation vs. fixed material in a single version.

7. Yes, because writers can use printed words to describe the oral experience; no, because essential aspects of the oral experience are impossible to re-create in a fixed text.

8. Sample questions: What specific oral forms are your favorites (for example, riddles, prayers, chants, charms, proverbs, stories, myths, folk tales, hymns)? Do you see any specific analogies between a particular Shakespearean passage and a selection from Native American literature?

## Susan Power

## Listening and Viewing, p. 7

Sample answers and guidelines for evaluation:

**Segment 1:** Susan Power claims that she began writing before she could read. Writing has always been an important part of her daily life. She began memorizing stories before she could read and loved listening to actors recite the dramatic works of Shakespeare. Students may describe certain books that were important to them as young readers and how they influenced their feelings toward reading and writing.

**Segment 2:** "Museum Indians" reflects on her relationship with her mother while growing up in Chicago; her mother took her to fascinating museums and libraries to make Susan feel at home in Chicago. Students may answer that Susan Power writes about cultural activities because she tries to explain Native American customs to others so that people will have a better understanding of the culture.

**Segment 3:** She listens to her words in order to hear the rhythm and sounds of words, which is a quality of Shakespeare's work that she admires. She also uses a tape recorder to listen to sentences while editing her writing. Students may answer that it is important to consider sound when writing so that the rhythm of the language is appealing to the audience; students may also suggest that rhythm and sound are important in poetry and plays but may not be as important in other types of writing, such as essays or nonfiction.

**Segment 4:** Susan Power hopes that she can bring her readers into a new, unfamiliar world and make it more familiar; she wants to expand her readers' experiences and make them aware of other beliefs and ways of life. Students may answer that they can learn more about differences in culture, history, and customs as well as tolerance.

**"The Earth on Turtle's Back"** (Onondaga)
**"When Grizzlies Walked Upright"** (Modoc)
*from* **The Navajo Origin Legend** (Navajo)
*from* **The Iroquois Constitution** (Iroquois)

## Literary Analysis: Origin Myths and Archetypes, p. 8

### Chart 1
### Sample Responses
#### "The Earth on Turtle's Back"

The World: The world is created when a muskrat dives to the bottom of the ocean, scoops up a tiny bit of Earth, and deposits it on the turtle's back. The Earth expands and becomes the whole world.

#### "When Grizzlies Walked Upright"

Mount Shasta: The Chief of the Sky Spirits carved a hole in the sky and pushed ice and snow down until he made a great mound, known as Mount Shasta, that reached from the earth almost to the sky.

Beaver, Otter, Fish, Birds: The Chief of the Sky Spirits broke off the end of his walking stick and threw the pieces into the rivers. The longer pieces turned into beaver and otter, and the shorter pieces became fish. The Sky Spirit blew upon leaves to turn them into birds.

Grizzly Bears: The Chief of the Sky Spirits made the grizzly bear from the big end of his giant stick.

#### from The Navajo Origin Legend

Man, Woman: The gods placed an ear of white corn, an ear of yellow corn, a white eagle feather, and a yellow eagle feather between two buckskins. Then the white wind and the yellow wind blew between them. After the Mirage People walked around the objects four times, the upper buckskin was lifted. The white ear of corn had been changed into a man, and the yellow ear had been changed into a woman.

### Chart 2

1. the muskrat from "The Earth on Turtle's Back"
2. the daughter of the Chief of the Sky Spirits from "When Grizzlies Walked Upright"
3. the Native American race from "When the Grizzlies Walked Upright"
4. corn from *The Navajo Origin Legend*

## Reading Strategy: Recognize Cultural Details, p. 9

### Sample Answers

1. The fact that the chief acts upon the dream of his wife shows that dreams hold a very important place in the lives of Native Americans.
2. They believed that a person should make up for any wrong he or she had committed.
3. People need to breathe air in and out in order to survive.

## Vocabulary Builder, p. 10

**A.** 1. recede
2. proceed
3. concede
4. deceased

**B.** 1. B; 2. D; 3. E; 4. C; 5. A

**C.** 1. A; 2. D; 3. B; 4. C; 5. B

## Grammar and Style: Coordinating Conjunctions, p. 11

**A.** 1. and; words
2. but; complete sentences
3. so; complete sentences
4. and; phrases
5. for; complete sentences

**B.** 1. The grizzlies looked as they do today, but they walked of two feet.
2. The daughter looked for the ocean, and she fell out of the mountain.
3. The little girl could die, or the grizzlies could save her.

## from The Iroquois Constitution by Dekanawidah

### Literary Analysis: Political Document and Symbols, p. 13

1. There are five nations in the Iroquois Confederacy.
2. The Tree symbolizes the foundation, or basis, of the Confederacy. It is meant to be strong and stand for the ideal of peace.
3. It demands that he pledge to the other lords his loyalty to the Constitution and to acting with justice.
4. They symbolize his pledge to the other lords and to the Constitution.
5. a guardian or protector, who warns them of danger
6. Students may suggest that the Iroquois people themselves must be watchful for signs of danger both within their own tribes and from outside.

### Reading Strategy: Analyze Author's Assumptions and Beliefs, p. 14

**Sample Answers**

1. He thinks the natural world is so valuable that any time the lords meet to discuss affairs, they must begin by giving thanks to the earth, the waters, the crops, and the animals.
2. He believes they must concern themselves only with serious matters, nothing trivial.
3. He thinks that young people's opinions are worth hearing; he cautions the lords not to ignore the criticisms of their nephews and nieces.
4. He assumes that they will make mistakes, but that if they listen to criticism they will return to the way of the Great Law.

## Vocabulary Builder, p. 15

**A.** 1. D; 2. F; 3. B; 4. A; 5. C; 6. E

**B.** 1. C; 2. D; 3. A; 4. B; 5. C; 6. B

## "A Journey Through Texas" from The Journey of Alvar Núñez Cabeza de Vaca by Alvar Núñez Cabeza de Vaca
## "Boulders Taller Than the Great Tower of Seville" by García López de Cárdenas

### Literary Analysis: Exploration Narratives/ Chronological Text Structure, p. 17

**Sample Answers**

1. The canyon was deep, and it was hard to find a way down. The trip down was difficult and long, and the men did not even reach the river at the bottom.
2. The Indians' estimate is correct, according to the narrative.
3. two days
4. They went all across the country until they reached the Gulf of Mexico, and the first part of the trip took seventeen days.

### Reading Strategy: Recognize Signal Words for Time, p. 18

1. five days
2. one day, or, the next day
3. two years in a row
4. They would cross uninhabited land before they reached the settlements, which were over twenty days away.
5. between 7 and 8 days
6. Women came with them with gourds filled with water, which they buried where the Indian travelers could find them.

### Vocabulary Builder, p. 19

**A.** Sample Answers
1. produce
2. projectile
3. progress
4. propel

**B.** 1. B; 2. B; 3. B; 4. D; 5. C; 6. B.

## from Of Plymouth Plantation by William Bradford

### Literary Analysis: Author's Purpose and Audience p. 21

**Sample Answers**

1. His audience is the following generations of the men who made the first voyage to Plymouth Plantation.

2. He wants to show the descendents of the colony that their fathers were both brave and frightened, but that they made the journey safely and under the protection of God.

3. He wishes to show readers the courage of some of the colony in caring for those who were ill, and to state that they will be rewarded by God.

4. He hopes to convince members of the audience that the hardships of the voyage brought out the best in some of the men, and through this to inspire his readers to continue the work of building the colony.

## Reading Strategy: Breaking Down Sentences, p. 22

**Sample Answers**

1. But [that which was most] <u>sad and lamentable was that in two or three months' time, half of their company died,</u> [wanting houses and other comforts;] <u>being infected with the scurvy and other diseases,</u> [which this long voyage and their inaccommodate condition had brought upon them,] <u>so</u> [as there died sometimes two or three of a day, in the foresaid time;] <u>that of one hundred and odd persons, scarce fifty remained.</u>

2. <u>But after they had sailed</u> [that course] <u>about half a day, they fell amongst dangerous shoals and roaring breakers,</u> [and they were so far entangled therewith as they conceived themselves in great danger; and the wind shrinking upon them withal, they resolved to bear up again for the Cape,] <u>and thought themselves happy to get out of those dangers before night overtook them,</u> [as by God's providence they did.]

3. [At length] <u>they understood</u> [by discourse with him] <u>that he was not of these parts, but belonged to the eastern parts, where some English ships came to fish, with whom he was acquainted,</u> [and could name sundry of them by their names,] <u>amongst whom he had got his language.</u>

## Vocabulary Builder, p. 23

**A.** 1. B; 2. A; 3. C
**B.** 1. B; 2. C; 3. A
**C.** 1. relent; 2. calamity; 3. adversity

## "To My Dear and Loving Husband" by Anne Bradstreet

## Literary Analysis: Puritan Plain Style—Syntax and Inversion, p. 25

**Sample Answers**

1. If there were ever two people who lived as one, we would be those people
   If there were ever a man who was loved by his wife, you would be that man.

2. short words

3. a wife's deep love for her husband

4. the word *persevere*

## Reading Strategy: Paraphrasing, p. 26

**Sample Answers**

1. If ever two people were united by love, then surely we are.

2. I value your love more than entire gold mines or all the riches of the Orient.

3. Let's love each other faithfully while we live So that when we die we may live forever in heaven

## Vocabulary Builder, p. 27

**A.** Sample Answers
1. With new farming methods, they increased food production tenfold.
2. There are multifold reasons for avoiding the sun when possible.
**B.** 1. recompense; 2. manifold; 3. persevere 4. quench
**C.** 1. C; 2. B; 3. C 4. C

## "Huswifery" by Edward Taylor

## Literary Analysis: Conceit (Extended Metaphor), p. 29

**Sample Answers**

1. a complete spinning wheel
2. his soul
3. the distaff, the part on which the wool is wound for spinning
4. a loom
5. God's glory

## Reading Strategy: Adjust Reading Rate, p. 30

**Sample Answers**

1. The poet is asking the Lord to make the poet himself into a spinning wheel. If the lines are read once slowly and then again, the meaning becomes clear.

2. I would read the lines once slowly. Then I would look at the bottom of the page to find the meanings of the unfamiliar terms. Then I would read the lines again with the knowledge of the unfamiliar words, which should make the lines easier to understand.

3. The second example can be read faster than the first. It is written in two short direct sentences. The first example puts the words in a somewhat unfamiliar order, which means that it should be read more slowly.

## Vocabulary Builder, p. 31

**A.** Sample Answers

1. False: If you have strong affections, your feelings are usually easy to see.

2. True: Marriage is a sacrament in many religious organizations.

3. True: A student shows good sense in doing homework before going to the movies.

4. False: People going outside in winter should wear warm clothing.

**B.** 1. affections; 2. apparel; 3. judgment; 4. ordinances

## *from* Sinners in the Hands of an Angry God
### by Jonathan Edwards

### Literary Analysis: Sermon, p. 33

**A. Sample Answers**

1. emotional

2. fear, terror, inferiority, self-loathing

3. pit of Hell; spider; loathsome insect; abhors you; worthy of nothing else but to be cast into the fire; abominable; hateful; venomous serpent; etc.

4. to come to Christ, to accept Christ in their lives

5. hope, relief, acceptance

6. extraordinary opportunity; Christ has thrown the door of mercy wide open; many are flocking to him, etc.

### Reading Strategy: Use Context Clues, p. 34

**Sample Answers**

1. "aware, able to perceive," since the context describes something the sinner (the person addressed) does not *see* and is unaware of

2. "angered; enraged," since the sentence is about God's *wrath*, or *anger*, and the word *provoked* parallels *incensed*

3. "to burn," since *flames* are performing the action and *burn* indicates a parallel action

4. "to refrain from; to stop," since God will not "lighten his hand" in the least and will show "no moderation or mercy"

5. "without limits; infinite," since the word modifies *duration* and we know there will be "no end" and the sinner shall experience "a long forever"

### Vocabulary Builder, p. 35

**A.** 1. C; 2. D; 3. B

**B.** 1. D; 2. F; 3. B; 4. E; 5. A; 6. C

**C.** 1. [circle A]; 2. [circle B]; 3. [circle B]

### Grammar and Style:
### Correlative Conjunctions, p. 36

**A.** 1. [circle *neither/nor*]; 2. [circle *either/or*]; 3. [circle *just as/so*]; 4. [circle *whether/or*]; 5. [circle *not only/but also*]

**B. Sample Answers**

1. *Not only* did Edwards terrify his congregation, *but* he praised the power of God.

2. *Just as* Edwards offered little hope of salvation to his flock, *so* did he condemn their unworthiness.

3. *Either* they accepted Jesus Christ in their hearts, he said, *or* they would burn in Hell.

4. The parishioners heard that they were condemned *whether* they led good lives *or* not.

5. Edwards said that *neither* good works *nor* personal holiness could save his listeners.

## "Speech in the Virginia Convention"
### by Patrick Henry
## "Speech in the Convention"
### by Benjamin Franklin

### Literary Analysis: Speeches, p. 38

**Sample Answers**

**Restatement:** "If we wish to be free, if we wish to preserve inviolate those inestimable privileges for which we have so long been contending"; "there is no peace. The war is actually begun. The next gale that sweeps from the north will bring to our ears the clash of resounding arms! Our brethren are already in the field!"

**Repetition:** "Let it come, I repeat, let it come"; the word *slavery* throughout; the word *peace* in the last paragraph

**Parallelism:** "We have petitioned; we have remonstrated; we have supplicated"; "Our petitions have been slighted; our remonstrances have produced additional violence and insult; our supplications have been disregarded"; "give me liberty or give me death!"

**Rhetorical Questions:** "Is this the part of wise men, engaged in a great and arduous struggle for liberty?" "Are fleets and armies necessary to a work of love and reconciliation?" "Can gentlemen assign any other possible motive for it?" "And what have we to oppose to them?" "Shall we try argument?"

### Reading Strategy: Evaluating Persuasive Appeals, p. 39

**Sample Answers**

1. Students may suggest that Henry is directing these words at the friendly audience members. He reminds them of values that they all share—a hatred of treason and of being disloyal to God's will.

2. Students may suggest that Franklin is directing these words at hostile audience members who are not happy with the Constitution. But even if they are not happy with the document, Franklin is showing them that the approval of the Constitution will confound their enemies, who are hoping the colonists will fail.

3. Students may suggest that Henry is directing these words at hostile audience members, who do not want to risk war with Great Britain. So Henry reminds them of the insults England has flung at the colonists and reminds them of one result of not forming a new nation —a British guard in every house.

## Vocabulary Builder, p. 40

**A.** 1. privilege; 2. despotism; 3. despot; 4. privileged

**B.** 1. unanimity; 2. vigilant; 3. subjugation;
4. privileges; 5. despotism; 6. sects

## The Declaration of Independence
### by Thomas Jefferson
### from *The Crisis, Number 1* by Thomas Paine

### Literary Analysis: Persuasion, p. 42

**Sample Answers**

1. **Emotional and logical appeals.** Paine uses the emotionally charged words *tyranny, hell,* and *glorious,* and he places himself on an equal basis with his audience by using the pronouns *us* and *we;* he also uses common-sense comparisons and cause-and-effect relationships in a logical chain of seemingly reasonable observations.

2. **Emotional appeal.** Paine places himself on an intimate level with his audience and compliments them as he calls them to action.

3. **Emotional and logical appeals.** Paine stresses the justness of the colonial cause by depicting it as a defensive war and uses the negatively charged words *thief, kills,* and *threatens* in a personal analogy with which most of his audience can identify, an analogy that appeals to his audience's sense of self-preservation and family responsibility. At the same time, he opens with a seemingly reasonable refutation of his distaste for an offensive war, and he then leads the audience through a logical chain of reasoning that summarizes his argument.

### Reading Strategy: Recognizing Charged Words, p. 43

**Sample Answers**

1. abuses, usurpations, despotism: These negative words emphasize the negative behavior of the British monarch and help arouse colonial indignation at his mistreatment.

2. wholesome, necessary, public good: These positive words stress the idea that the colonial position is perfectly justified and nobly motivated.

3. oppressions, humble: The words, one negative and one positive, stress the contrast between Britain's insensitivity and the colonies' laudable behavior.

4. tyranny, hell: These negative words emphasize the negative behavior of the British monarch and help arouse colonial indignation at his mistreatment.

5. warm ardor, friend: These positive words stress the nobility of the colonial cause and appeal to colonial loyalties.

### Vocabulary Builder, p. 44

**A.** 1. rectify
2. fortitude

3. erect
4. solitude

**B.** 1. honest; 2. yes; 3. cautious; 4. justice; 5. nod;
6. honor; 7. bother; 8. absolute ruler

## "To His Excellency, General Washington"
### by Phillis Wheatley

### Literary Analysis: Personification and Heroic Couplets, p. 46

**Sample Answers**

**A.** 1. Earth is personified as a mother who gave birth to the American colonists.

2. The nations of the world are personified as people capable of gazing at scenes and being unfamiliar with them.

3. The speaker's pen is personified as the writer of the lines; some students may also note that the poet's Muse, whom she addresses directly, is a personification of the abstract idea of poetic inspiration, further personified as being capable of bowing.

4. Autumn is personified as a monarch enjoying a golden reign.

**B.** A crown, a mansion, and a throne that shine,

With gold unfading, WASHINGTON! be thine.

### Reading Strategy: Reread to Clarify Meaning, p. 47

**Sample Answers**

5. While freedom's cause disturbs her anxious breast.
1. See mother earth grieve for her children's fate.
2. Where the unrolled flag waves high in [the] air.
3. Shall I sing their praise to Washington?
4. Hear every tongue beg you for your protection.
5. When America's fury found French powers.
6. While the rising hills of dead grow larger around us.
7. And their combined music floats through the air.

### Vocabulary Builder, p. 48

**A.** 1. favorable; 2. disturbance; 3. military; 4. beg;
5. mourn; 6. thoughtful

**B.** 1. before taking a test; 2. a loss by the school team;
3. a hurricane; 4. a general's uniform; 5. a snowstorm;
6. a friend to borrow a DVD

## from The Autobiography and from Poor Richard's Almanack by Benjamin Franklin

### Benjamin Franklin: Author in Depth, p. 50

1. B; 2. C; 3. C; 4. A; 5. B

## Literary Analysis: Autobiography, p. 51

**Sample Answers**

1. At the beginning of his attempts at moral perfection, Franklin is confident that he can succeed. He is also determined and willing to try.
2. Franklin is surprised that success eludes him.
3. Franklin is confident that a week's time will be sufficient to cure himself of a particular bad habit.
4. Franklin is surprised that moral perfection is harder to achieve than he had thought.
5. He believed in getting things done and not wasting time.
6. He thought it best to forget those who wronged him and remember those who were his friends.

## Literary Analysis: Aphorisms, p. 52

**Sample Answers:**

1. You should do things when they need to be done and not postpone them.
2. Let insults and hurts go, but hold on to kindnesses.
3. You are never too old to learn.
4. It is impossible to keep a secret as soon as you tell it to another person.
5. Doing good work is more valuable than talking about it.
6. Improvement comes only with hard work.
7. It is important to value and keep your true friends.
8. It is easier to heal from a small injury, but you may never overcome having said something you shouldn't have.

## Reading Strategy: Cause-and-Effect Relationships, p. 53

**Sample Answers**

1. CAUSE: More virtues with fewer ideas; EFFECT: Clearness
2. CAUSE: Virtue of order was difficult; EFFECT: Almost gave up
3. CAUSE: Attaining a perfect character; EFFECT: Earning the hatred of friends
4. CAUSE: Pains; EFFECT: Gains
5. CAUSE: Haste; EFFECT: Waste

## Vocabulary Builder, p. 54

**A.** Sample Answers:

1. state of being watchful
2. state of excessive watchfulness

**B.** 1. B; 2. E; 3. D; 4. C; 5. A; 6. F

**C.** 1. B; 2. C; 3. A

## Grammar and Style: Subordinating Conjunctions, p. 55

1. Before he started his project    [circle *Before*]
2. because he had so much trouble with the virtue of Order    [circle *because*]

3. As Franklin discovered a fault in himself    [circle *As*]
4. until he had achieved perfection    [circle *until*]
5. Since his scraping put holes in his books    [circle *Since*]
6. If your head is wax, don't walk in the sun.    [*circle If*]

## Literary Analysis: Companing Autobiograph, p. 57

**Sample Answers**

1. Similar: Both talk about endeavoring to do something important and having some form of success. Both are happy with where they are in their lives.

   Different: Franklin's language is formal; he writes without reference to others. Cisneros's language is informal. She includes references to others in her writing.

2. Similar: Franklin set up a method to help him become more virtuous. Cisneros realized she had to know the steps involved in becoming a writer if she were to become a good one.

   Different: Franklin's language is formal and complex. Cisneros's language is informal and conversational

## Vocabulary Builder, p. 58

**Sample Answers**

**A.** 1. old music; 2. forbidden; 3. sees it in his or her head; 4. grow well; 5. efficient

**B.** 1. A; 2. B; 3. C; 4. B; 5. C

### From the Scholar's Desk

## William L. Andrews Introduces *The Interesting Narrative of the Life of Olaudah Equiano* by Olaudah Equiano, p. 60

1. It is astonishing that history has preserved almost no firsthand accounts of the Middle Passage. This fact makes Equiano's narrative a rare, detailed report.
2. In composing the narrative, Equiano would almost inevitably have to have relived his suffering and the anguish of others.
3. The first stop is the ship's suffocating hold, where conditions are "loathsome." The "human cargo" is forced to stand for most of the transatlantic voyage. On the deck, Africans are dying of the illnesses they have contracted in the hold. The European crew merely watches and waits, indifferent to the captives' suffering.
4. They sympathize with the ten-year-old African narrator, feeling his shock and dread. They are alienated from the brutal whites.
5. According to Andrews, Equiano's peek into the quadrant gives him a glimpse of an unimagined world and arms him with a resilience and inquisitiveness that will allow him to survive. Evaluations of Andrews's claim will vary.

**William L. Andrews**

## Listening and Viewing, p. 61

Sample answers and guidelines for evaluation:

**Segment 1:** William L. Andrews first became interested in studying African American history and culture by growing up in the segregated South; African Americans were part of his world but also separated from his world, which made him curious to learn more about their culture. Andrews acts as a middle man by pointing out the relevance of these nineteenth-century writings to people today.

**Segment 2:** Olaudah Equiano was a slave who purchased his own freedom and became a shrewd businessman. He wrote a book about his experiences coming to America on a slave ship and overcoming tremendous odds; this book became the foundation for all slave narratives. Students may answer that slave narratives are firsthand accounts written by slaves or former slaves about their experiences. Students may suggest that slave narratives are important to society because they offer a personal, intimate account of significant historical events that occurred during the nineteenth century, and they provide a different perspective than do traditional history books.

**Segment 3:** William L. Andrews researches primary sources when writing about historical figures of the past because he wants to learn as much as possible about the person, reading documents written by people who were personally and directly involved with the subject. Students may suggest that they could offer insights into the writer's life and personality that may provide further understanding of the description of events in the narratives and could also verify factual details.

**Segment 4:** Slave narratives often tell stories that have the "common denominators" of emotion, hardship, and humanity that all readers can relate to in their own lives. Students may answer that readers can learn from Equiano's narrative because it shows the diversity that exists in the world and allows the reader a greater perspective for interaction in today's global world.

## *from* The Interesting Narrative of the Life of Olaudah Equiano by Olaudah Equiano

## Literary Analysis: Slave Narratives, p. 62

**Sample Answers**

1. They might imagine the situation and feelings of the slaves and realize that the practices of slavery and slave trading were neither morally nor legally acceptable.

2. They made their money from selling the slaves at the end of the journey. The more people they crowded into the hold, the more money they would make.

3. Olaudah points out that the slavetraders lost many potential "sales" to the sickness and death of the slaves, so their greed was [shortsighted]. By overfilling the hold, they hoped to make more money. Instead, many slaves died, and they lost money.

4. merchant's custody; we were sold; buyers rush at once; that parcel they liked best

5. Answers will vary. Be sure students address the elements in the question.

## Reading Strategy: Summarizing, p. 63

**A. Sample Answers**

**Main Idea:** The traders mistreated their captives. Key Supporting Details: tossed fish overboard rather than feed it to the captives; when captives tried to get fish, they were flogged

**Main Idea:** Equiano, in spite of the hardship, finds time to think about sailing on the ocean. Key Supporting Details: mentions flying fishes; first sees quadrant used

**Main Idea:** The captives are landed at Barbados and sold into slavery. Key Supporting Details: merchants and planters inspect captives; captives bewildered, terrified; old slaves let captives know what will happen—they won't be eaten but will be put to work

**B. Sample Answer**

Equiano and his fellow captives are crammed aboard a ship under terrible conditions: crowded, smelly, disease-ridden. Their captors treat them cruelly, and many slaves perish. Despite the hardships, Equiano does take note of his first experience of sailing the ocean, mentioning such things as flying fish and the use of a quadrant. When he and his fellow slaves arrive in Barbados and are inspected by prospective buyers, they are quite terrified until older slaves explain that they will not be eaten but put to work.

## Vocabulary Builder, p. 64

**A.** 1. inject
2. ejected
3. project
4. rejected

**B.** 1. B; 2. D; 3. C; 4. E; 5. A

**C.** 1. antonyms; 2. antonyms; 3. synonyms;
4. syonyms; 5. antonyms; 6. antonyms

## "Letter to His Wife" by John Adams
## "Letter to Her Daughter from the New White House" by Abigail Adams

## Primary Source: Letters, p. 66

1. The main difference is that John Adams does not attempt to describe the house, and Abigail has many descriptions of it. In this period, it was a wife's role to pay attention to the house and keep it up.

2. Perhaps John Adams doesn't know much about architecture and doesn't know how to describe a building. Or, perhaps he doesn't want to prejudice Abigail before she sees the house.

3. Some students may suggest that the comparison is humorous, since John thinks the building "is in a state to

be habitable," meaning "it can be made fit to live in," and Abigail says "the house is made habitable but there is not a single apartment finished," which appear to be a contradiction. Clearly, the Adams' were less than thrilled at their first view of the White House. Some students may not find the comparison humorous, but depressing, because the White House was to be the house of the President of the nation, and it was in need of so much work.

4. Abigail Adams was not a whiner or a complainer, she was a doer. She recognized the poor state of the house she was to live in as the wife of the President, and she immediately began thinking about how she could improve it.

## Vocabulary Builder, p. 67

**A.** 1. B; 2. C; 3. B; 4. D; 5. A; 6. C; 7. B; 8. D; 9. A
**B.** 1. interspersed
2. unabated
3. scale
4. recourse
5. contract
6. establishment

# Unit 2

## Names and Terms to Know Worksheet, p. 69

**A. (Possible responses)**
1. huge tract of land in what is now central U.S. sold by Napoleon to the U.S.
2. seventh U.S. President, champion of the "little man"
3. thousand+ mile forced trek of Cherokee from Georgia to Oklahom
4. most popular "Fireside Poet"
5. poet Walt Whitman's description of his style
6. women's rights convention organized in 1848 in New York state

**B. (Possible responses)**
1. Technology such as steamships and canals made transportation easier and faster. Other inventions like the telegraph improved communication and spurred productivity on the farm and factory. Americans became more prosperous and were able to communicate and travel much faster.
2. Geographic expansion impelled white settlers to move into what had been Indian lands; the government forced the Indians to move farther west.
3. Transcendentalism, shaped by Ralph Waldo Emerson and Henry David Thoreau, provided a backbone for the American belief in the individual's ability to rise above brute reality to a higher ideal.

## Essential Question Worksheet, p. 70

**A. (Possible responses)**
1. a. the natural wonders and expanse of their country
   b. waterfalls, mountains, canyons, fertile plains, forests

2. a. Americans found many types of resources to develop for economic gain.
   b. It inspired reverence and awe.
3. a. The woods and mountains of upstage New York were the settings for the fantastic stories of Irving and the Leatherstocking Tales of Cooper.
   b. Hawthorne, Melville, Poe, Emerson, Thoreau, Whitman, Dickinson
   c. naturalist Audubon; painter Cole of the Hudson River School; Olstead who designed Central Park

**B. (Possible responses)**
1. my history teacher
2. colorful, elevated vocabulary, elegant sentences
3. They would be pleased, because it would allow them to sell more goods..

## Essential Question Worksheet, p. 71

**A. (Possible responses)**
1. a. steamships, cotton gins, telegraph
   b. To ease and speed communication and transportation of people and make the production of goods more productive
   c. More people lower down on the social scale acquired more political power in the Age of Jackson. There was agitation for rights of women and abolition of slavery.
   d. Half of the nation still sanctioned slavery. Women could not vote.
   e. the states where people were allowed by law to hold slaves had built their economies on slave labor. These states comprised the southern half of the nation.
2. a. British novels by Scott and Dickens
   b. Harriet Beecher Stowe and her best-selling *Uncle Tom's Cabin* and Fireside poet Henry Wadsworth Longfellow
3. a. They wanted to improve American society and spread democracy; to define a "public self" for Americans.
   b. Hawthorne, Melville, Poe, Irving
   c. real truths lay outside sensory experience

**B. (Possible responses)**
1. something about the writer's feelings and life
2. we saw amazing national parks
3. with confidence and without seeking much help

## Essential Question Worksheet, p. 72

**A. (Possible responses)**
1. a. informality, use of slang, conversational style, colorful vocabulary, lack of fancy diction
   b. sitting for a spell, taking a fork in the road
   c. He wrote in a "barbaric yawp" that sounded conversational, used both plain and elegant words, foreign and native ones.
2. a. James Fenimore Cooper's Leatherstocking Tales, folktales, stories about real-life Daniel Boone and Davy Crockett
   b. Melville's Captain Ahab, Hawthorne's Hester Prynne

c. It was an individualist who sought to reach a feeling of oneness with all the is beautiful and good.

3. a. moving westward with the frontier

b. optimism, belief in human goodness

c. humans are driven toward self-destructiveness, guilt, and cruelty

d. It expressed American confidence and the ability to persist against all odds to form a new culture.

**B. (Possible responses)**

1. Technology makes it easier for them to communicate and travel to each other.

2. the right to free speech

3. People are likely to be optimistic and materialistic.

## Follow-Through Activities p. 73

### A. Check Your Comprehension

Guidelines: Students should complete the chart with other concepts appropriate to the period and the groups that are associated with these concepts.

### B. Extend Your Learning

Guidelines: Students should complete the chart with answers that will help them to research a form of spoken literature from the early period of American history.

### "The Devil and Tom Walker"
by Washington Irving

## Literary Analysis: Characterization, p. 74

1. H; 2. A; 3. F; 4. B; 5. C; 6. E 7. D; 8. G

## Reading Strategy: Evaluate Social Influences of the Historical Period, p. 75

### Sample Answers

1. In the early 1700s, husbands and wives apparently shared the household as common property.

2. Intolerance of religious attitudes was prevalent during this era, an era that also saw many Americans engaged in the slave trade and some involved in witch hunts—all behavior that Irving considers "of the devil."

3. People believed that God used nature to punish them, as in earthquakes.

4. Greed was very much a part of life in New England, at least in Irving's eyes. Irving is warning them in this story about Tom Walker.

## Vocabulary Builder, p. 76

**A.** 1. export; 2. extrovert; 3. exhale; 4. exoskeleton.

**B.** 1. A; 2. D; 3. C; 4. B; 5. B; 6. A

## Primary Sources Worksheet, p. 78

### Sample Answers

1. Lewis says: "This morning I . . . dispatched Drewyer and the Indian down the river." This fulfills Jefferson's

statement that "The object of your mission is to explore the Missouri river."

2. Lewis describes a meeting between Sah-ca-ga-we-ah and an Indian woman, both of whom had been taken prisoner by the Minnetares. This tells us that some tribes took women as prisoners and that some women were able to escape, fulfilling Jefferson's order that Lewis find out about the Indians' "relations with other tribes or nations."

3. Lewis describes a fork in the river with a "level smooth bottom covered with a fine turf of green-sward." This fulfills Jefferson's order to "take observations . . . at all remarkable points on the river."

4. Lewis describes a meeting with some Indians, in which he "apprised them of the strength of our government and its friendly dispositions towards them." This fulfills Jefferson's order to "make them acquainted with the position, extent, character, peaceable and commercial dispositions of the United States; of our wish to be neighborly, friendly, and useful to them."

## Vocabulary Builder, p. 79

### Sample Answers

**A.** 1. B; 2. C; 3. A

**B.** 1. practicable
   2. latitude, longitude
   3. discretion
   4. dispatched
   5. conspicuous
   6. prospect
   7. conciliatory
   8. membrane
   9. celestial

### "The Song of Hiawatha" and
### "The Tide Rises, The Tide Falls"
by Henry Wadsworth Longfellow
### "Thanatopsis" by William Cullen Bryant
### "Old Ironsides" by Oliver Wendell Holmes

## Literary Analysis: Meter, p. 80

The metrical pattern has lines of iambic tetrameter alternating with lines of iambic trimeter.

Oh, bet|ter that| her shat|tered hulk
   Should sink| beneath| the wave;
Her thun|ders shook| the might|y deep,
   And there| should be| her grave;
Nail to| the mast| her hol|y flag,
   Set eve|ry thread| bare sail,
And give| her to| the god| of storms
   The light|ning and| the gale!

## Reading Strategy: Summarizing to Repair Comprehension, p. 81

**Sample Answers**

1. Death unites all people no matter their status in life.
2. It would be better if she (the ship Old Ironsides) were sunk at sea with dignity by a storm.

## Vocabulary Builder, p. 82

**A.** 1. C; 2. A; 3. B

**B.** Replacement words are underlined.

1. The valleys were blanketed in a <u>pensive</u> quietness.
2. The sky was filled with <u>innumerable</u> birds flying overhead.
3. The ravages of time will soon <u>efface</u> the letters on the monument.
4. The speaker's <u>eloquence</u> moved the audience to tears.

## "The Minister's Black Veil"
Nathaniel Hawthorne

## Literary Analysis: Parable and Symbol, p. 84

**Sample Answers**

1. The simple description of the villagers sounds like people everywhere: The children behave like most children, and the bachelors behave like most bachelors.
2. No name is given to the deceased. The point is not *who* the deceased was, but the way that the other people responded to her death.
3. The language of this excerpt focuses on the veil and speaks of it in strong and symbolic language.

## Reading Strategy: Draw Inferences to Determine Essential Meaning, p. 85

1. Students may know that wearing a veil like this is not normal, and that a minister is assumed to be close to God. As a result, students may infer that the veil represents a division between Hooper and God.
2. Students will probably understand how busybodies like to interfere with other people's lives. As a result, they may infer that something very significant has happened to make Hooper different and unapproachable about the veil.

## Vocabulary Builder, p. 86

**Sample Answers**

**A.** 1. Pathology is concerned with the causes, prevention, and treatment of disease.
2. No, I would not. If I felt antipathy toward another person, I would dislike that person intensely.
3. If a friend suffered a terrible disappointment, I would show that I was sympathetic by putting a comforting arm around him or her.

**B.** 1. Because of Megan's obstinacy, she was never willing to change her mind—not even if there were good reasons.
2. Everyone had great respect for the venerable old man.
3. The inanimate object stayed in one place, not moving.
4. The audience was moved to tears at the pathos in the play.
5. The impertinent child showed no respect to his elders.
6. The sound of the hummingbird's wings was imperceptible from twenty feet away.

## Grammar and Style: Using Adjective and Adverb Clauses, p. 87

**A.** 1. <u>As the people approached the meetinghouse</u>, the sexton tolled the bell.
adverb clause modifying the verb *tolled*
2. Mr. Hooper, <u>who walked slowly toward the meetinghouse,</u> was wearing a veil.
adjective clause modifying the noun *Mr. Hooper*
3. Mr. Hooper gave a powerful sermon <u>while the parishioners wondered about the veil</u>.
adverb clause modifying the verb *gave*
4. The veil, <u>which was made of black crape</u>, covered most of Mr. Hooper's face.
adjective clause modifying the noun *veil*
5. <u>After he performed the wedding ceremony</u>, Mr. Hooper raised a glass to his lips.
adverb clause modifying the verb *raised*

**B.** Sample Answers

1. When the visitors were seated in Mr. Hooper's home, they felt very uncomfortable.
adverb clause modifying the verb *felt*
2. Elizabeth, who had been engaged to him for some time, asked him to remove the veil.
adjective clause modifying the noun *Elizabeth*
3. As she hinted at the rumors surrounding the veil, Elizabeth began to cry.
adverb clause modifying the verb *began*
4. The guilt that Mr. Hooper suffered caused him great sorrow.
adjective clause modifying the noun *guilt*
5. The veil, which he refused to remove, was buried with him.
adjective clause modifying the noun *veil*

## "The Fall of the House of Usher" and "The Raven" by Edgar Allan Poe

## Poe Biography, p. 89

**Sample Answers**

**A.** Part I Summary: Alone in the world, Poe was taken in by the family of John Allan, living with them in England till age eleven.

Suggested visual: Poe and the Allan family on a ship that is coming into port in England

Part II Summary: After joining the army at age 18, Poe published two volumes of poetry. His military career ended when he was expelled from West Point for bad grades.

Suggested visual: Poe in an army uniform writing poetry by candlelight

Part III Summary: Unable to make much money from his poetry, he turned to fiction and literary criticism. His work began to gain him some recognition.

Suggested visual: The window of an 1840s bookstore with Poe's works on display

Part IV: Summary: Poe's final years were marked by poverty, depression, and madness. He died two years after the death of his beloved wife, Virginia.

Suggested visual: Poe, distraught, tending to his sick wife

**B.** 1. Being raised by people who never adopted me made me feel like an outsider, as did being expelled from West Point. These feelings come out in my work. Many of my characters do not have normal human relationships.

2. I think that any reader who enjoys mysteries, vivid imagery, unusual characters, and gothic literature will be drawn to my stories and poems.

3. Distinctly American qualities include an independent spirit and an openness to new experiences. My writing shows both, for I invented the detective story, and my psychological thrillers are like no others.

## Literary Analysis: Single Effect, p. 90

**Sample Answers**

1. A. high, narrow, pointed windows
   B. feeble light
   C. "an atmosphere of sorrow"
2. A. the oppressive air
   B. its darkness, dampness, and depth
   C. the grating door
3. A. the light of the storm and of the moon
   B. the widening fissure
   C. the sound of its cracking
4. A. his unusual appearance
   B. his feverish conversation
   C. his odd books
5. A. her pathetic illness
   B. her ghastly passage through Usher's room
   C. her bloodied appearance

## Literary Analysis: Gothic Style, p. 91

**Sample Answers**

**A.** 1. Setting: a cemetery in 1850
2. Character: a man who is mourning the death of his wife
3. Events: The distraught husband visits the grave of his wife, who had been buried earlier that day. In his

grief, he throws himself across the gravesite. As he lies there on the ground, he hears a faint sound from below. It sounds like a scratching. He convinces himself that she is still alive in the coffin, scratching at the lid. He digs up the earth with his bare hands and opens the coffin. It turns out she'd been in a coma so deep that it looked like death (to a doctor in 1850 whose technology didn't measure faint signs of life) and has just revived.

4. Phrases: pounding heart, frantic digging, bloody fingernails

**B.** 1. An air of "irredeemable gloom hung over and pervaded all."
2. "it was in the bleak December"
3. the lady Madeline being put alive into the tomb
4. The narrator has a "soul with sorrow laden."

## Reading Strategy: Break Down Long Sentences, p. 92

1. Suggested core sentence: I had been passing alone through a singularly dreary tract of country and found myself within view of the melancholy House of Usher.

Sample clarification: Traveling alone through a dreary area, I came within view of the melancholy House of Usher.

2. Suggested core sentence: I reined my horse and gazed down upon the inverted images of the gray sedge, and the ghastly tree stems, and the vacant and eyelike windows.

Sample clarification: I reined my horse and looked at the gloomy reflection [in the tarn] of the house and landscape.

3. Suggested core sentence: He admitted that much of the peculiar gloom which thus afflicted him could be traced to the severe and long-continued illness—indeed to the evidently approaching dissolution—of a tenderly beloved sister.

Sample clarification: He admitted that a lot of his gloom was caused by the fatal illness of his beloved sister.

4. Suggested core sentence: Our books were in strict keeping with this character of phantasm.

Sample clarification: Our books were consistent with our eerie state.

## Vocabulary Builder, p. 93

**A.** Sample Answers

1. When you *advocate* something, you use your voice in support of it.
2. *Vocabulary* refers to the words we know and speak.
3. Something *evocative* calls forth memories or images in our minds.

**B.** 1. B; 2. C; 3. A; 4. C; 5. C; 6. C; 7. B; 8. C; 9. B

## Grammar and Style: Comparative and Superlative Adjectives and Adverbs, p. 94

**A.** 1. superlative; 2. superlative; 3. comparative;

4. comparative
**B.** Sample Answers
1. more difficult
2. most surprising
3. dreariest
4. more cheerful
5. most peculiar
6. bleakest
7. more loudly
8. most ominously
9. most frightening
10. more effective

## Literary Analysis: Comparing Gothic Literature
### p. 96

Students should note that both passages describe aspects of the exterior of a residence. Both discuss features that show deterioration. They are different in that the Poe excerpt describes the outside of a building that is in a state of disrepair, and the Oates excerpt describes a swing set that is in disrepair.

## Vocabulary Builder, p. 97
**A.** 1. B; 2. C; 3. A; 4. B
**B.** 1. B; 2. C; 3. D; 4. D; 5. A

## *from* **Moby-Dick** by Herman Melville

### Literary Analysis: Symbol, p. 99
**Sample Answers**
1. Starbuck may represent the voice of reason and religious faith; both are overridden by Ahab's obsession.
2. The sea may represent the overwhelming forces of nature that overpower humanity and its efforts, represented by the ship; the sea may represent Ahab's fanatical, irrational obsession (or fanaticism or obsessive behavior in general), which destroys human society or the spirit of community, represented by the ship.
3. The sky hawk may represent heavenly faith and innocence, which like the crew is destroyed by Ahab's fanatical, obsessive behavior.

### Reading Strategy: Identify Relevant Details, p. 100
**Sample Answers**
1. the "peculiar mark" of his walk, his "ribbed and dented brow" with its "still stranger footprints" of "his one unsleeping, ever-pacing thought"
2. thought; a warped nature; brooding; obsession; vengeance
3. his footprints; the imprints of his one good leg and one ivory peg
4. comparing the planks with those prints to geological stones; calling the mark of his walk "peculiar," connect-

ing the imprints on the planks to the imprint on his mind "of his one unsleeping, ever-pacing thought" (of vengeance against the whale)
5. obsession; vengeance; Ahab's warped, obsessive nature

## Vocabulary Builder, p. 101
**A.** 1. D; 2. B; 3. B; 4. A; 5. C
**B.** 1. D; 2. C; 3. A; 4. B; 5. F; 6. E

## Grammar and Style: Using Participles, Gerunder, and Infinitives, p. 102
**A.** 1. infinitive phrase
2. participial phrase
3. participial phrase
4. gerund phrase
5. infinitive phrase
6. participial phrase
**B.** Sample Answers
1. <u>Standing on the deck,</u> Ahab was a formidable figure. (participial phrase)
2. Ahab's sole purpose was <u>pursuing the whale.</u> (gerund phrase)
3. Ahab wanted <u>to take revenge.</u> (infinitive phrase)

## *from* **Nature,** *from* **Self-Reliance,** and **"Concord Hymn"**
### by Ralph Waldo Emerson

## Literary Analysis: Figurative Language, p. 104
1. metaphor; 2. imagery or synecdoche; 3. imagery;
4. metaphor; 5. synecdoche; 6. imagery;
7. synecdoche; 8. description.

## Reading Strategy: Challenging, or Questioning, the Text, p. 105
**Sample Answers**
1. Society is the enemy of individualism; society forces people to conform.
2. Students should recognize that, following the opening sentence of the paragraph, the next three sentences constitute evidence. They will probably feel that these sentences do not offer strong support because they consist merely of additional assertions and are basically restatements of the opening assertion in different words.
3. Support: laws that limit freedoms; peer pressure to conform

   Refute: laws that protect freedoms; notice and sometimes admiration given those who are different

## Vocabulary Builder, p. 106
**A.** Sample Answers
1. shining out in rays, or as if in rays

2. a line coming from the center of a circle like the spoke of a wheel
3. a heating device sending out rays of heat
4. an appliance that sends out or picks up messages broadcast like rays through the air, or air waves
5. emitting energy in waves or rays

**B.** 1. C; 2. B; 3. C; 4. D; 5. C; 6. A

## Contemporary Commentary

## Gretel Ehrlich Introduces from *Walden* by Henry David Thoreau, p. 108

1. She grew up on the central California coast.
2. Examples include Thoreau's opinions about land and home ownership, about the relative importance of wealth or poverty, and about life lived on a moment-by-moment basis.
3. A. Details include the changing weather, changing human relationships, physical changes in our bodies, and the cycle of natural change.
   B. Sample responses: Yes, because nature is always developing, growing, and changing; no, because human beings ought to hold onto certain fundamental principles that do not change.
4. Thoreau would have us simplify, slow down, become quiet, and try to reach the heart of things.
5. He means the fresh, dawn-like character of things—in other words, their essence in the here and now.
6. Sample responses: Yes, because our individuality is our most precious asset; no, because cooperation, harmony, and interdependence are sometimes essential.
7. Sample questions: Was Thoreau ever apprehensive or agitated when he was living at Walden Pond? What happened to Thoreau after his stay at Walden Pond was over?

## Gretel Ehrlich

## Listening and Viewing, p. 109

**Segment 1:** Gretel Ehrlich believes that, since we come from super-materialistic America, we may not have a concept of what other people are like. Traveling provides insight into the way others live and deal with hardships and, most important, helps an individual develop compassion. Students may suggest that these experiences afforded them opportunities to learn about different people and places and gain a new understanding of humanity.

**Segment 2:** Gretel Ehrlich structured her book that describes her experiences in Greenland like Thoreau's *Walden;* the book chronicles the writer's experiences during the four seasons. Ehrlich also lived off the land in Greenland and Wyoming for many years, much the way Thoreau lived close to nature at Walden Pond.

**Segment 3:** Gretel Ehrlich thinks that writing is a fresh rendition of an experience, character, or observation; it is crucial to take notes in order to have details to expand into

a story. Students may say they use scraps of paper, notebooks, journals, outlines, computers, etc.

**Segment 4:** Gretel Ehrlich believes that the writer must contribute something to society that is worth reading and has universal appeal and value. Students may suggest that by reading anthropological books, they would appreciate the common bonds of humanity and learn to tolerate the differences.

## *from Walden* and *from Civil Disobedience* by Henry David Thoreau

## Literary Analysis: Style, p. 110

**Sample Answers**

1. Word choice: Thoreau uses fairly simple words sprinkled with an occasionally complex, formal term, such as *auroral, terrestrial, celestial.*
2. Sentence length: Thoreau uses fairly long sentences in this passage.
3. Sentence type/structure: Thoreau tends to use long simple or compound sentences lengthened by several verbal and prepositional phrases. He varies sentence beginnings by opening one sentence with a prepositional phrase.
4. Rhythm: Thoreau achieves a quiet, regular rhythm in this descriptive passage.
5. Literary devices: Thoreau uses fairly vivid images and figurative language, such as "airy and unplastered cabin," "broken strains . . . of terrestrial music", and the comparison of the cabin to a place "where a goddess might trail her garments."

## Reading Strategy: Analyze the Author's Implicit and Explicit Philosophical Assumptions, p. 111

Students may cite some of the following main ideas: Simplify your own life and concentrate on what is truly meaningful. Value your own life, no matter how poor it may seem. Dare to be a nonconformist. Be wary lest you serve only the needs of the few. Use civil disobedience, if necessary, to make your government more responsive to individual needs.

Students should cite or summarize different portions of the selections to support each main idea and then list personal experiences that support or refute the main idea. Analysis of each main idea should take into account students' personal experiences.

## Vocabulary Builder, p. 112

**A.** 1. C; 2. A
**B.** 1. A; 2. B; 3. C; 4. B; 5. A; 6. B

## Emily Dickinson's Poetry

## Literary Analysis: Rhyme and Paradox, p. 114

**A.** 1. see/me, exact; 2. chill/Tulle, slant; 3. Despair/Air, exact; 4. I, Fly, internal

**B.** The paradox is that the speaker refers to two deaths that preceded her final death. This seems impossible until you consider that she might be talking about the death of her heart, or having her heart broken so badly that life had no meaning after that.

## Reading Strategy: Rereading to Monitor and Repair Comprehension, p. 115

### Sample Answers

1. It has been centuries since then, yet it feels shorter than the day I first thought the horses were heading in the direction of eternity.
2. The brain is deeper than the sea, for if you hold them side by side, the brain will be able to absorb, or understand, the sea, just as sponges can absorb the water in buckets.
3. Space, the sea, and death might seem like solitude, but they will really seem like society

## Vocabulary Builder, p. 116

**A.** Sample Answers

1. to limit a word to a particular meaning; to provide the limits of a word's meaning
2. to redo the outer limits, or outside, of something (such as a piece of furniture)
3. ending (as of a piece of music)

**B.** 1. surmised; 2. infinity; 3. oppresses; 4. finite; 5. ample; 6. affliction

**C.** 1. C; 2. D; 3. B; 4. B

### Walt Whitman's Poetry

## Literary Analysis: American Epic Poetry, p. 118

### Sample Answers

1. This passage expresses Whitman's belief in the interconnectedness of all humanity. He felt that each person was a part of every other person's life.
2. This passage shows the connections between generations, with each generation having the same value.
3. This passage lists various kinds of workers, giving each one the same degree of dignity and worth.
4. In this passage, the speaker is feeling a kinship with all the soldiers who are sleeping in the tents.
5. This passage puts all the mentioned workers on an even plane, each one singing a different song, all equally inspiring.

## Reading Strategy: Infer the Poet's Attitude, p. 119

Students should select passages that they had to read slowly, explain why they slowed down, and explain the meaning of the passage.

### Sample Answers

Passage: "A noiseless patient spider, / I mark'd where on a little promontory it stood isolated . . ."

Why I Slowed Down: The word order is unusual, I wasn't sure of the meaning of the multiple-meaning word *mark'd*, and I had to look up the word *promontory*.

Meaning of Passage: I watched a little spider where it stood alone on a high point of land.

## Vocabulary Builder, p. 120

**A.** 1. C; 2. A; 3. B; 4. D

**B.** 1. I depart as air, I shake my white locks at the runaway sun, I *pour out* my flesh in eddies, and drift it in lacy jags.

2. Creeds and school in *temporary suspension*, retiring back a while sufficed at what they are, but never forgotten.

3. In the history of earth hitherto the largest and most *active* appear tame and orderly to their ampler largeness and stir.

4. I *hand down* myself to the dirt to grow from the grass I love . . .

5. . . . as I lift my eyes they seem to be *secretively* watching me.

6. . . .at night the party of young fellows, *healthy*, friendly, Singing with open mouths their strong melodious songs.

# Unit 3

## Names and Terms to Know Worksheet, p. 123

**A. (Possible answers)**

1. The attack on Fort Sumter by Confederate forces was the start of the Civil War.
2. The Homestead Act of 1862 offered 160 acres to anyone who would work the land.
3. the 1880s and 1890s, when cities grew, lit by electric lights and the economy expanded
4. fictional character who went from rags to riches by working hard
5. Civil War novel by Stephen Crane
6. type of writing focusing on unique features of local areas, usually rural

**B. (Possible responses)**

1. The Civil War lasted over four years, and it divided families. The North took advantage of its industrial nature. The agrarian South, where most of the war was fought, was devastated..
2. The Age of Electricity gave Americans both brighter and dirtier streets. Electricity made work easier, but the resulting industrial growth accelerated pollution, led to urban blight, and exploited immigrant and child labor.
3. The Homestead Act and the growth of railroads encouraged Americans to settle the West. As settlements expanded, Indians were driven out of their lands to "reservations." As more land was developed into farms, the frontier disappeared.

## Essential Question Worksheet, p. 124

**A. (Possible responses)**

1. a. Spirituals were hymns sung by slaves, using work rhythms and Biblical imagery. They communicated the woe of the enslaved life and the hope for a freedom and happiness in heaven.

   b. Frederick Douglass's autobiography; Mary Chestnut's journal

   c. corruption and incompetence among businesses and industries

2. a. of the rise of the hard-working, poor boy Horatio Alger to wealth through "luck and pluck"

   b. the unpredictability of life

   c. Zane Grey westerns and Frank Baum's *Wizard of Oz*

3. a. The violence of the Civil War disillusioned Americans and made them lose their optimism.

   b. recognizable details of everyday life as lived by ordinary people, shown in an honest factual way

   c. Edward Arlington Robinson and Edgar Lee Masters

   d. describing the powerlessness individuals in the face of an indifferent univers

**B. (Possible responses)**

1. I would feel very sad.

2. the attacks on September 11, 2001

3. a palace

4. because you have strong feelings for that family member and want him or her to win

## Essential Question Worksheet, p. 125

**A. (Possible responses)**

1. a. believe that what was bigger and stronger was better

   b. urban problems, such as the emotions and values of people crowded into cities

2. a. The war left it devastated, with homes and plantations destroyed and the cotton economy, which depended on slavery, in ruins.

   b. rural areas

3. a. the unique details of life in particular American settings, usually rural or small town

   b. Mark Twain; southern writers such as Kate Chopin; northerner Sarah Orne Jewett

   c. Henry James, Edith Wharton, William Dean Howells

**B. (Possible responses).**

1. difficult, because of its great change

2. unpleasant, because he or she would be unhappy and posibly complaining

3. fear, because it would control people's actions

4. a park, because an idyll has a natural setting

## Essential Question Worksheet p. 126

**A. (Possible responses)**

1. a. uniquely American settings such as Civil War battle-fields, the Yukon, a riverboat

   b. common speech and dialect

   c. expose human weakness

2. a. tried to describe the world in objective terms

   b. They depicted local settings in realistic detail.

   c. European influences included Darwin, Marx, and Zola

   d. heredity, environment, and social conditions

3. a. hard-edged pragmatism

   b. war tarnished by shame, fear, and guilt

   c. a man crushed by nature

   d. ordinary, everyday people

   e. fascination with science and a belief in progress

**B. (Possible responses)**

1. a frog

2. won't wear light blue

3. had heard it many times before

4. she always saw simple, practical solutions to problems

## Follow-Through Activities p. 127

### A. Check Your Comprehension

Guidelines: Students should complete the chart with other concepts appropriate to the period and the groups that are associated with these concepts.

### B. Extend Your Learning

Guidelines: Students should complete the chart with answers that will help them to research a form of spoken literature.

## "An Occurrence at Owl Creek Bridge"
### by Ambrose Bierce

## Literary Analysis: Point of View, p. 128

### Sample Answers

1. How unbelievable! Here I am not far from home, standing on a bridge, about to die. The river is swift, sparkling, just twenty feet down there. My hands hurt. They tied them too tightly with that rough cord. And the rope . . . the rope around my neck is prickly. Soon it will tighten and tighten. What will it be like? How quickly will death come?

2. As the man fell through the bridge, the watching soldiers swayed back slightly, as if they had all inhaled simultaneously and might hold their breath until he died. He did not die immediately; as he dangled in the air he seemed to come to life, if only for a short time.

## Reading Strategy: Identify Chronological Order, p. 129

### Sample Answers

1. The "preternatural" sensory experience suggests the heightened sensations some people believe occur just before death.

2. The whirling Farquhar does here might suggest the turning of a body at the end of a rope.

3. The scene is not natural. The large road seems untraveled, and there is no sign of life anywhere.

## Vocabulary Builder, p. 130

**A.** 1. the highest good; 2. with highest praise

**B.** 1. summarily
   2. dictum
   3. ineffable
   4. etiquette
   5. deference
   6. apprised

## Primary Sources: War Correspondence, p. 132

### Sample Answers

1. Were these people truly enjoying the prospect of a war?
2. Chesnut says that for once in her life she listened. How good of an observer can she be?
3. Why does Goss begin his journal in such a cheerful manner?
4. What is Goss preparing to do? Go to war? Go courting?
5. Why did Goss think it would be okay to speak to the drill sergeant like this?
6. What lesson has Goss learned from these experiences?
7. Why were the soldiers ordered to attack under these circumstances?
8. Will the men succeed against such overwhelming odds?

## Vocabulary Builder, p. 133

1. The *recruits* did not know how to march.
2. The enemy *intercepted* a letter that was begin sent to headquarters.
3. The officers failed to make a decision, so they *adjourned* the meeting.
4. The soldiers stayed in *entrenchments* in order to avoid being shot.
5. The *brigade* prepared for battle.
6. The general was *obstinate* and wouldn't give up the fight.
7. A *spectator* stood on the distant hill.
8. Citizens held a *convention* to talk about ways they could help the wounded.
9. The battle showed a marked *fluctuation* throughout the day.
10. The commander told the officers to plan an *offensive*.

## "An Episode of War" by Stephen Crane

## Literary Analysis: Realism and Naturalism, p. 134

### Sample Answers

1. Naturalism: The event of being shot is a force beyond the lieutenant's control.

2. Naturalism: This passage emphasizes the lieutenant's and the women's reactions to an event outside their control; Realism: The reaction reflects realistic responses to the lieutenant's injury.

## Reading Strategy: Recognize Historical Details, p. 135

1. **War tactics:** Most battles were hand-to-hand combat, making injury likely.
2. **Medicine:** Medicine was less advanced, and wartime hospitals were short on staff and supplies, increasing the chances that an injury would become life threatening. The lieutenant's injury turns into an amputation, whether necessary or not.
3. **Communication:** Letters to families took a long time, particularly during wartime. When the lieutenant returns home, his family does not know about his amputation.
4. **Transportation:** Soldiers moved by horse or by foot. Injured men could not be rushed to an emergency room. The lieutenant has to bring himself to the field hospital, which probably made his condition worse.

## Vocabulary Builder, p. 136

**A.** 1. gregarious; 2. egregious; 3. congregation; 4. aggregation

**B.** 1. A; 2. C; 3. B; 4. D

**C.** 1. A; 2. C; 3. B

## *from* My Bondage and My Freedom
by Frederick Douglass

## Literary Analysis: Autobiography and Tone, p. 138

### Sample Answers

1. The effects are strength and self-knowledge. Writing this as an autobiography makes the writer seem more real and the passage more convincing. The tone is one of insistent reasonableness and honesty that invites readers to believe his story.
2. In this passage, the perceptions and effects are pain and despair. Describing images such as a "dragon ready to pounce" from a first-hand viewpoint draws the reader into Douglass's horror at being enslaved. The tone is one of careful analysis and controlled resentment that reinforces the experience he is relating by making it sound authentic.
3. The effects of this passage are anger and sorrow. By using the first person, Douglass demonstrates anger, rather than merely reporting it. The tone is one of controlled anger, reinforcing feelings natural to his experience.

## Reading Strategy: Establish a Purpose, p. 139

**Sample Answers**

**Character:** Mrs. Auld's eventual brutal opposition to Douglass's efforts to learn to read

**Ethical influence:** She became educated in the cultural ethics of slavery that convinced her that educating slaves was bad and dangerous and responded in the manner of people of the time.

**Characters:** small boys with whom Douglass talked about slavery and who sympathized with him

**Ethical influence:** The boys naturally thought of him as a person; they were not yet governed by the slave mentality that possessed many Southern adults of the period.

**Incident:** Douglass's reluctance to identify the boys who helped him learn to read because they might be embarrassed

**Ethical influence:** During those times, helping a slave learn to read was both illegal and unethical. It might also suggest a weakness of character or intelligence, so these helpers might be embarrassed.

## Vocabulary Builder, p. 140

**A.** 1. beneficiary; 2. benign; 3. beneficent; 4. beneficial

**B.** 1. C; 2. F; 3. D; 4. A; 5. B; 6. E

## "Swing Low, Sweet Chariot" and "Go Down, Moses" Spirituals

## Literary Analysis: Refrain, p. 142

**Sample Answers**

1. "Swing low, sweet chariot,/Coming for to carry me home" or "Coming for to carry me home"

2. The allegory in "Go Down, Moses" refers, on the literal level, to Moses freeing the Israelites who were held in bondage in Egypt. On a symbolic level, it refers to slaves in the South—the Israelites symbolizing the slaves and Egypt symbolizing the South.

3. The allusion to Jordan refers to the River Jordan in the Near East that is mentioned in the Bible. Crossing the Jordan represents crossing into freedom in the spiritual.

4. Their repetition increases the intensity and the urgency of the spiritual's message.

5. The refrains in both spirituals refer to the desire for freedom. In "Swing Low, Sweet Chariot," the refrains refer to a release—that of death and going to Heaven. In "Go Down, Moses," the refrains are couched as a demand for freedom during life. The refrains in "Go Down, Moses" are much more militant than those of "Swing Low, Sweet Chariot."

## Reading Strategy: Listen, p. 143

**Sample Answers**

**"Swing Low, Sweet Chariot"**

Cell 1. In second verse *see* and *me* rhyme

Cell 2. "Swing low, sweet chariot" and "Coming for to carry me home"

Cell 3. yearning or longing

Cell 4. Encourages patience and faith in eventual freedom from hardship

**"Go Down, Moses"**

Cell 1. "Pharaoh" and "go"; "land" and "stand"; "said" and "dead"

Cell 2. "Go down, Moses," "Way down in Egypt land," "Tell old Pharaoh," "To let my people go"

Cell 3. persistence and determination

Cell 4. Eventually the powerless will triumph over the powerful.

## Vocabulary Builder, p. 144

**A.** 1. suppress
2. express
3. pressurize
4. press
5. impression
6. depression

**B.** 1. B; 2. A

**C.** 1. E; 2. C

## "The Gettysburg Address" by Abraham Lincoln
## "Letter to His Son" by Robert E. Lee

## Literary Analysis: Diction, p. 146

1. A; 2. B; 3. A; 4. B; 5. B; 6. A; 7. A; 8. A

## Reading Strategy: Use Background Knowledge, p. 147

**Sample Answers**

1. Lee admired Washington and his policies, and had a great love for his country.

2. Lee's earlier freeing of his slaves demonstrated his willingness to act on principles, regardless of their popularity.

3. Lee was a patriot who had served the United States in its army for a long time.

## Vocabulary Builder, p. 148

**A.** 1. bless; 2. honor; 3. chaos; 4. atonement

**B.** 1. C; 2. B; 3. A; 4. A

## Contemporary Commentary

## Nell Irvin Painter Introduces "An Account of an Experience with Discrimination" by Sojourner Truth, p. 150

**Sample Answers**

1. Sojourner Truth served with a volunteer group of anti-slavery women who helped poor people from the battlefields of Virginia and from slaveholding Maryland.

2. She told how one streetcar conductor had not stopped for her and how another conductor had tried to push her from the platform of the car.

3. The first American history is that of Washington, D.C., a Southern city. The second American history is that of discrimination against African Americans throughout the United States.

4. It was national in scope because racial discrimination was national.

5. Frederick Douglass: traded blows with conductors who tried to push him out of his seat. Harriet Tubman: suffered shoulder injuries when she was dragged out of her seat and thrown into the baggage car. Frances Ellen Watkins Harper: experienced humiliating conflicts on streetcars and railroads.

6. Sample questions: What kinds of source material do you find most useful? What areas of research would you recommend to a young historian today?

## Nell Irvin Painter

## Listening and Viewing, p. 151

Sample answers and guidelines for evaluation:

**Segment 1:** Nell Irvin Painter's interest in history developed while she studied abroad in France and Africa and began to ask herself questions about her own country's history. Students may answer that historians write about significant events and people of the past. Their writings are important to society because they explain, clarify, and analyze past events for a modern-day audience.

**Segment 2:** Sojourner Truth was a preacher, an abolitionist, and a feminist who became an important national symbol during the Civil War. Nell Irvin Painter wants her audience to know that Truth was born and raised in New York, which was then a slave state. She also did not say "Aren't I a woman?" at a convention, as she has been famously quoted for over a century.

**Segment 3:** Primary sources are documents that are intimate to an event and the people directly involved in the event; they are often more personal, emotional, and detailed than sources written by people many years later. These sources are important to Nell Irvin Painter's work because the information in her book must be as accurate as possible.

**Segment 4:** Nell Irvin Painter believes that it is important for students not to take the first thing they are told as fact but instead to look at it critically, realizing that there are many layers and that history is much more complicated. Students may answer that they can learn more about a historical event or era and get a more personal, intimate account of history from a different perspective.

## "An Account of an Experience with Discrimination" by Sojourner Truth

## Literary Analysis: Author's Purpose and Tone, p. 152

### Sample Answers

1. Truth's purpose is to inform readers about an incident of discrimination. Her purpose is clear because she gives specific, precise information about the incident, such as whom she was with and what exactly she was doing when the incident occurred.

2. Truth's tone is measured and calm, factual but not inflammatory. Words such as "I ascended the platform," "the conductor pushed me," and "I told I was not going off" are matter of fact, not passionate or angry.

3. Neither the author's purpose nor tone change in the course of the report. Truth's purpose throughout is to inform readers, and her language remains the same.

## Reading Strategy: Identify Relevant Details and Facts, p. 153

### Sample Answers

1. conductor of a streetcar; refused to stop his car for me
2. dismissed him; take the number of the car whenever I was mistreated
3. get a ride without trouble; with another friend
4. conductor pushed me; "Go back—get off here."
5. "Does she belong to you?"; "she belongs to humanity."
6. hard for the old slaveholding spirit to die; die it must.

## Vocabulary Builder, p. 154

**A.** 1. Sojourner Truth *ascended* the steps to enter the streetcar.

2. The conductor denied that he had made an *assault* against Truth.

**B.** 1. A; 2. D

## "The Boys' Ambition" *from* Life on the Mississippi and "The Notorious Jumping Frog of Calaveras County" by Mark Twain

## Twain Biography, p. 156

### A. Sample Answers

**Life on the River:** Grew up along the Mississippi; loved it so much he took his pen name from a river boatman's term; became a riverboat pilot at a young age. Photograph: Mississippi River steamboat.

**A Traveling Man:** Traveled west and worked as journalist; his first story, "The Notorious Jumping Frog of Calaveras County," made him famous; Used his Western adventures and childhood on the Mississippi as ideas for his books. Photograph: Jumping frog contest in the Old West.

**A Restless Soul:** Traveled widely in his later years; lost his wife and three children; became pessimistic about people and society. Photograph: Twain giving a lecture before a crowd of people in Great Britain.

### B. Sample Answers

**Twain:** No, I wasn't really serious, but you know the Mississippi always meant a lot to me. There's so much interesting life along that river—people and places—and of course it's always changing. Spending life as a riverboat pilot would have been a good life, a fascinating life.

**Twain:** Humor is at the heart of my writing. It's not the most important thing, perhaps, but the rest of it, all the ideas and people, would have been empty and dull creations without the humor.

**Twain:** Americans are impossible to define. There is every kind of person in America. You'll find the finest, most principled characters and the most flawed and ridiculous characters right here. That diversity is what makes Americans and this great country such a fascinating place for an observer of human nature to live.

## Literary Analysis: Humor, p. 157

1. dialect and sense of human foibles
2. dialect, hyperbole, sense of human foibles
3. dialect
4. dialect
5. incongruities

## Reading Strategy: Understand Regional Dialect, p. 158

### Sample Answers

1. He was so strange about betting that he would bet on anything. He would even bet the opposite of his original bet if he couldn't persuade anyone else to.
2. Smiley had a mare. Others called the mare the fifteen-minute nag, but only to tease. They called her that because naturally she was faster than that. Smiley used to win money by betting on that horse, even though she was slow and always seemed to have something wrong with her.
3. The dog didn't look like he was worth much. You wouldn't expect the dog to do much except lie around, look mean, and wait for a chance to steal something. But as soon as someone bet money on that dog, he seemed to become another dog entirely. His jaw would stick out like the front of a steamboat does, and his teeth would suddenly show and shine like the steamboat's burning furnaces.
4. Suddenly he would grab the other dog by the joint of its hind leg. He would freeze his jaw on that leg, not biting or chewing on it, but just gripping and hanging on. He

would hang on until people stopped him, even if it took a year.

## Vocabulary Builder, p. 159

**A.** 1. monolingual; 2. monoplegia; 3. monosyllable; 4. monosomic

**B.** 1. D; 2. G; 3. A; 4. F; 5. C; 6. B; 7. E

## Grammar and Style: Fixing Misplaced and Dangling Modifiers, p. 160

**A.** 1. The steamboat that arrived at the landing was the first that day; steamboat
2. Waiting his turn, the man inspected the frog carefully; man
3. The gentlemen stood lost in thought; gentleman
4. Looking carefully at his frog, he realized something was wrong; he
5. The man who got the last laugh knew better than to stay around town; man

**B.** 1. Laughing heartily, the crowd cheered for the winning frog.
2. Correct
3. Eager to see the steamboat arrive, the boys left their chores undone.
4. Correct
5. He often exaggerated stories while he was working as a reporter.

## *from* The Life and Times of the Thunderbolt Kid by Bill Bayson

## Literary Analysis: Humor, p. 162

1. human foibles
2. regional behavior
3. human foibles, hyperbole
4. incongruity
5. hyperbole, human foibles

## Vocabulary Builder, p. 163

**A.** 1. commence; 2. questionable
**B.** 1. D; 2. A

## "To Build a Fire" by Jack London

## Literary Analysis: Conflict, Setting, Irony, p. 165

1. external; person against nature; setting is central; no irony
2. internal; person against himself; setting is not central to conflict; ironic because he is trying to contain his fear but situation is serious.

3. external; person against another character; setting is not central to the conflict; ironic because the dog senses the severity of the situation as well as the man does

4. external; person against nature; setting is central; ironic because readers know the fire represented safety but this accident will lead to disaster

5. external; person against nature; setting is central; no irony

6. external; person against himself; setting is not central; ironic because running will not save him

7. external; person against fate;; setting is not central; no irony

## Reading Strategy: Draw Inferences and Make Predictions, p. 166

Students should cite specific clues from setting, predictions based on those clues, and the actual outcomes from the text. For example, Clue: . . . [the dog] experienced a vague but menacing apprehension that subdued it and made it slink along at the man's heels . . .; Prediction: the man may not realize how dangerous the cold really is; Outcome: the dog's instincts were correct.

## Vocabulary Builder, p. 167

**A.** Sample Answers

1. *Depend* means to hang down or from something else. Going to the cabin hangs upon the weather.

2. *Appendix* is a section of a book that extends from the end of the book. Special words are often put in the appendix at the end.

3. To *suspend* something is to hang something from something else. You might suspend, or hang, a bird feeder from a branch.

**B.** 1. C; 2. D; 3. D; 4. C 5. C

## Grammar and Style: Using Introductory Phrases and Clauses, p. 168

**Sample Answers**

**A.** 1. To build a fire in the snow and bitter cold, he worked carefully.

2. When he called to it, the dog avoided him.

3. When he called to it, he knew he could not survive.

4. In the warm cabin, his friends stayed warm and thought about their friend on the trail.

5. After his feet became soaked in the cold stream, he had to act quickly to save his life.

**B.** 1. Because he was alone in the wilderness, the traveler relied upon his dog.

2. On such bitter cold days, experienced Alaskans stayed inside.

3. With his matches gone, he could not build a fire.

4. When the snow put out the fire, he nearly panicked.

5. To keep warm, he walked quickly along the trail.

**"Heading West"** by Miriam Davis Colt
**"I Will Fight No More Forever"** by Chief Joseph

## Primary Sources: Memoir and Speech, p. 170

**Sample Answers**

1. The assumption is that farming implements will not be available where they are going.

2. The assumption is that travel by steamboat is dangerous.

3. The assumption is that the Georgians supported slavery and that they were dangerous if they found someone among them who did not support that view.

4. The assumption is that houses and businesses would be built, that the town would be much further along toward thriving.

5. The assumption is that his children were unprepared and have had a hard time trying to survive.

## Vocabulary Builder, p. 171

**A.** 1. T; Shares represent portions of ownership.

2. F; A levee is an embankment built to prevent flooding.

3. T; A foothold is a secure position from which they could grow stronger.

4. F; A prairie is a grassland.

5. T; *Forded* means "crossed the river at a low point."

**B.** 1. There were *emigrants* from many lands in the West.

2. As far as the eye could see, the prairie was covered by a *profusion* of wild flowers.

3. The feeling *pervading* the Nez Perce camp was despair.

4. The people followed a *ravine* until they came to some water.

5. The settlers *surveyed* before they built their homes and settled the land.

**"The Story of an Hour"** by Kate Chopin

## Literary Analysis: Irony, p. 172

1. Situational irony: Students should choose a passage that illustrates how the outcome of an action or a situation is different from what the reader expects.

2. Dramatic irony: Students should choose a passage that illustrates how the reader is aware of something that a character in the story does not know.

## Reading Strategy: Relate the Work to Major Themes of the Era, p. 173

Students may cite various details from the story and should relate them to themes or issues that reflect the concerns of the period. Two examples follow:

Detail: Mrs. Mallard is troubled by the death of her husband, but in the end, becomes relieved and almost joyful as she looks forward to spending the rest of her life independent of him.

Issue: She represents a growing unrest among women of the era who sought greater independence.

Detail: The narrator describes the typical marriage as one in which the man, no matter how much he loves his wife, will exerts his will and dominate her.

Issue: The traditional relationship of husband and wife is being questioned.

## Vocabulary Builder, p. 174

**A.** 1. A; 2. C; 3. B; 4. D

**B.** 1. repression
2. tumultuously
3. forestall
4. elusive

## "Douglass" and "We Wear the Mask"
### by Paul Laurence Dunbar

## Literary Analysis: Formal Verse, p. 176

1. *abbaabba*
2. *cdcdcd*
3. *aabba*

## Reading Strategy: Interpret, p. 177

### Sample Answers

1. The "we" stands for African Americans. Some students may think it stands for all honorable people who value freedom.
2. Students will probably answer that it is the public sentiment on African Americans' position in society.
3. The "shivering bark" is the African American people as a group.
4. The "lonely dark" is the hard times the African Americans are living in.
5. He addresses it to Douglass because Douglass was known as a fighter for freedom for all African Americans.
6. The mask is hiding the true feelings of African Americans.
7. The cheeks and eyes must be hidden so that no one can see the true emotions of African Americans.

## Vocabulary Builder, p. 178

**A.** 1. *beguiled* (misled by deceit or craftiness)
2. *guileless* (innocent or naive, not exposed to guile)
3. *beguiler* (one who misleads by deceit or craftiness)
4. *beguiling* (misleading by deceit or craftiness)

**B.** 1. A; 2. D; 3. A; 4. B; 5. C

## "Luke Havergal" and "Richard Cory"
### by Edwin Arlington Robinson
## "Lucinda Matlock" and "Richard Bone"
### by Edgar Lee Masters

## Literary Analysis: Speaker, p. 180

### Sample Answers

1. The speaker must be a ghost, because he or she speaks "out of a grave."
2. It is likely that the woman is dead, since messages about her are brought by one who speaks from the grave, and because she can only be reached through leaves that whisper or by listening to the wind.
3. The speaker seems to be providing advice about a supernatural journey, one that would make it possible to contact a woman who cannot be contacted in the physical world. The meeting or contact Havergal seeks is likely to be supernatural, because the woman will call him "if [he] trusts her." The leaves cannot physically whisper to Havergal, and a kiss cannot be literally flaming on his forehead. In addition, the speaker is a ghost, and would seem to be more qualified to speak about the supernatural than the natural.
4. No, the speaker advises Havergal that "there is not a dawn in eastern skies/To rift the fiery night that's in your eyes," and that "the dark will end the dark, if anything," suggesting that there is no hope for Havergal, and that the only route he can take is a "bitter" one.
5. Something terrible must have happened to Luke Havergal, leaving him with a "fiery night" in his eyes. The speaker advises Havergal on how to contact or reunite with the woman he seeks or misses, so perhaps Havergal was separated from the woman, possibly by her death. It's possible that Havergal may have done something terrible, such as contributing to the woman's death, because the speaker seems to feel that there is no hope for him. The speaker may be suggesting that Havergal meet his death willingly.

## Reading Strategy: Comparing and Contrasting, p. 181

### Sample Answers

"Luke Havergal": *aabbaaaa* rhyme scheme, iambic pentameter; third-person point of view; loss of a loved one.

"Richard Cory": *abba* rhyme scheme, iambic pentameter; third-person point of view; suicide and how little we know of the troubles of others.

"Lucinda Matlock": unrhymed iambic pentameter; first-person; living and loving life fully.

"Richard Bone": unrhymed iambic pentameter; first-person; the parallels between life as it is and life as we wish it to be.

## Vocabulary Builder, p. 182

**A.** 1. existing at birth
  2. kind or type of literature
  3. of the original kind
  4. the people born at a certain time
**B.** degenerate, repose, epitaph, chronicles

### "A Wagner Matinée" by Willa Cather

## Literary Analysis: Characterization, p. 184

1. Clark thinks his Aunt Georgiana's appearance is unsightly.
2. Aunt Georgiana was not an outwardly beautiful woman.
3. Aunt Georgiana eloped with her husband and moved with him to the Nebraska frontier, thus avoiding local criticism of her for marrying him.
4. Aunt Georgiana looked out for Clark when he was a boy.
5. Aunt Georgiana had lost something (music) that she loved very much.
6. The concert was an emotional experience for Aunt Georgiana.
7. Aunt Georgiana's hands, which once played the piano so well, are now deformed because of hard work.
8. Aunt Georgiana does not want to leave the life she remembers in Boston for her life in Nebraska.

## Reading Strategy: Clarify, p. 185

**Sample Answers**

1. A chilblain is a painful swelling or sore caused by exposure to cold.
2. The trip started in Red Willow County, Nebraska, and ended in Boston, Massachusetts.
3. The Green Mountains are in Vermont.
4. Aunt Georgiana had been a music teacher at the Boston Conservatory years earlier.
5. Venusberg is a legendary mountain in Germany where Venus, the Roman goddess of love, held court.
6. It reminded her of a young man she knew who used to sing the song.

## Vocabulary Builder, p. 186

**A.** 1. nonmusical
  2. nonmusical
  3. musical
  4. musical
**B.** 1. overture; prelude
  2. with a quivering voice; tremulously
  3. unable to move; inert
  4. light-hearted joking; jocularity
  5. very respectful; reverential

# Unit 4

## Names and Terms to Know Worksheet, p. 189

**A. (Possible answers)**

1. President of the U.S. during World War I, elected in 1912
2. the right of women to vote
3. group of public programs developed by Franklin D. Roosevelt to help Americans cope with the Great Depression
4. U.S. naval base location, where Japanese planes attacked on December 7, 1941
5. a 5-part poem by T. S. Eliot expressing the sickness with modern life
6. 1920s cultural flowering in Harlem, the largely African-American area in New York City

**B. (Possible answers)**

1. The "can-do" progressive spirit of the early 1900s gave way to a sense of waste and hopelessness as a result of the bloody war.
2. The New Deal permanently expanded the U.S. government and its involvement in the lives of ordinary Americans. It gave people a sense of hope, as they found work in public projects.
3. World War II further expanded the government, ended U.S. isolation from the rest of the world forever, turned American into the world's most powerful nation, and brought the country into the atomic age, when it dropped atomic bombs on Japan.

## Essential Question Worksheet p. 190

**A. (Possible responses)**

1. a. The cities became centers of culture; they also grew uncontrollably and had large poor and immigrant populations.
   b. smaller; drought in the 1930s
2. a. Americans no longer believed as strongly in the nobility of Western culture; they felt disaffected from society.
   b. entry into a more sophisticated modern age
3. a. They were young people whose youth was blighted by World War I, who sought escape in the hedonism of the roaring 20s.
   b. Eliot and Fitzgerald
   c. African-American culture and modern urban life
   d. Sinclair Lewis; Eudora Welty and William Faulkner

**B. (Possible responses)**

1. no, because a metropolis is a city.
2. because he or she is away from home, permanently
3. because it is full of stupid reality shows

## Essential Question Worksheet p. 191

**A. (Possible responses)**

1. a. the old values didn't work in the modern world

   b. The Depression made more Americans poor; the New Deal gave them work.

   c. the Holocaust and atomic bombs

2. a. useless to prevent the bloodshed and waste of World War I

   b. women, African Americans, and immigrants

   c. brought about by the war and the stress of modern urban life.

3. a. linear narrative in fiction, orderly meters and rhyme schemes in poetry

   b. Gertrude Stein, Harriet Monroe

   c. Langston Hughes

   d. Stories and poems were organized in unconnected bursts or moments.

   e. movies, radio, pulp fictin

**B. (Possible answers)**

1. Disillusion is likely to make someone less happy, because it means that your beliefs have been discredited.

2. everybody is so busy that we eat different foods at different times

3. home and kindergarden

## Essential Question Workshop, p. 192

**A. (Possible responses)**

1. a. They left out transition; did not always follow chronological order; left plotlines unresolved and forced readers to figure things out for themselves.

   b. Modernists explored unstated, implied themes.

   c. They used a journalistic, more flat style, fewer flowery descriptions.

   d. images and allusions from various cultures, present and past, all over the world

2. a. it was difficult to figure out what they meant

   b. Readers became used to the Modernist conventions, as writers taught they how to read in the modern way.

3. a. They felt the world was without meaning; they were spiritually exhausted.

   b. self-indulgence, escapist, expatriate; Fitzgerald and Hemingway

   c. the good, ordinary person who remains close to the land; Faulkner and Welty

   d. Wallace Stevens, Ezra Pound, William Carlos Williams, E.E. Cummings, Marianne Moore, Robert Frost

   e. Langston Hughes, Claude McKay, Countee Cullen, Zora Neale Thurston

**B. (Possible responses)**

1. easy to find because it is everywhere

2. Ambiguity makes things less clear.

3. inventing or imagining something new

## Follow-Through Activities p. 193

### A. Check Your Comprehension

Guidelines: Students should complete the chart with other concepts appropriate to the period and the groups that are associated with these concepts.

### B. Extend Your Learning

Guidelines: Students should complete the chart with answers that will help them to do their research.

## "The Love Song of J. Alfred Prufrock"
### by T. S. Eliot

### Literary Analysis: Dramatic Monologue, p. 194

**Sample Answers**

1. The women are intelligent and educated. Michelangelo was a famous painter, so if the women spoke of him, they had to be at least somewhat educated.

2. From earlier parts of the poem, it is clear that Prufrock is attending a party. These lines show how afraid he is of the social situation. He seems to want to turn back. Perhaps he is fearful of seeing the woman he secretly loves and being frustrated by his inability to express his feelings.

3. Prufrock seems to be afraid of the judgments people make about him. He feels like an insect that a scientist has impaled on a pin and is studying in a cold, analytic way. These lines may show his fear of revealing his true self when the world seems to "have him pegged."

4. He would like to be more daring and unconventional ("Shall I part my hair behind?"), enjoy sensual pleasure ("dare to eat a peach"), be more casual and enjoy nature and life ("wear white flannel trousers, and walk upon the beach").

### Reading Strategy: Adjust Reading Rate, p. 195

**Sample Answers**

1. The repetition of *yellow, rubs, window-panes* forces the reader to pay attention to the nonrepetitive elements and imparts a sense of expectation that the pattern will continue.

   The imagery of *rubs its back, rubs its muzzle* gives a visual picture of the fog as a cat-like animal, which draws out the first syllables of the first words. The repetition of these words gives the lines rhythm.

2. The alliteration of *t's* and *d's* forces syllables to be stressed, and that produces the meter of the lines. Repetition of the word *time* and the phrase *Do I dare?* forces the stress on these elements. The rhyme of *dare/stair/hair* (masculine rhyme) stresses these words, supporting the metric pattern.

3. The rhyme of *flicker/snicker* (end rhyme) produces emphasis to the musical effect. The repetition of *I have seen* slows the meter.

## Vocabulary Builder, p. 196

**A.** 1. cut it apart; 2. taken away; 3. different from the others; 4. turn away from it; 5. break apart

**B.** 1. malingers; 2. meticulous; 3. obtuse; 4. insidious; 5. digress

## Poems by Ezra Pound, William Carlos Williams, and H. D.

### Literary Analysis: Imagist Poems, p. 198

1. red wheelbarrow, rainwater, white chickens
2. Sample answer: rain, lights, figure 5, gold, red.
3. Sample answer: Most of the objectives of the Imagist poets are achieved in this excerpt: the language is certainly of the everyday variety, no clichés are used, the rhythms are unique and new, the choice of subjects is unusual, the image is concrete, and the language is concentrated. Perhaps the only objective that is not achieved is that of suggesting rather than stating directly, unless the plums are seen as a symbol of something else.

### Reading Strategy: Engage Your Senses, p. 199
**Sample Answers:**

"Metro" (Touch, "wet");

"wheel barrow" (Sight, "white chickens");

"Figure" (Sound, "gongs");

"Just to Say" (Taste, "sweet");

"Pean Tree" (Sight, "flower-tufts")

### Vocabulary Builder, p. 200

**A.** 1. apparent; 2. apparition; 3. appearance
**B.** 1. voluminous; 2. dogma; 3. apparition

## "Winter Dreams" by F. Scott Fitzgerald

### Literary Analysis: Characterization, p. 202

1. In Dexter's mind, anything was attainable.
2. The already rich may have been squandering their wealth, but Dexter's quest for riches makes him determined in his business.
3. Dexter's financial success reflects that of many people after World War I: People who had been the servants became the served.
4. Judy's ideas about love and affection are influenced by a need for wealth.

### Reading Strategy: Draw Inferences to Determine Meaning, p. 203
**Sample Answers**

1. Sometimes Dexter behaves impetuously.
2. Judy probably does not feel sorry about it, and perhaps feels she has been inconvenienced by hitting him.

3. The fact that Judy does not go out of her way to impress Dexter reveals that she does not consider him to be important.
4. Dexter seems to be ashamed of his background.
5. Judy uses her physical attractiveness to cause men to want her and probably forgive her for anything she does.

### Vocabulary Builder, p. 204
**Sample Answers**

**A:** 1. Her mother subsidized her small business.
2. a sedentary life style is unheal they.
3. To vote, you must be a state resident.
4. He is assiduous in studies and music.

**B.** 1. B
2. D
3. A
4. B
5. C
6. A

### Grammar and Style: Subject-Verb Agreement Problems, p. 205

**A:** 1. attends
2. plan
3. looks
4. changes
5. is

**B.** 1. Incorrect; First one caddy and then all the others ask to caddy for Mr. Hart.
2. Incorrect; Only four balls that were hit by the novice golfer are found.
3. Correct.
4. Incorrect: There are many ways to succeed in life.
5. Incorrect; Dexter thinks too much before he makes a decision.

## "The Turtle" *from* The Grapes of Wrath by John Steinbeck

### Literary Analysis: Allegory and Theme, p. 207
**Sample Answers**

1. Story detail: The turtle crawls over the grass, "turning aside for nothing."

   How it connects to theme: Like the Joads, the turtle has a goal—to get across the road—and he won't be deterred.
2. Story detail: "A red ant ran into the shell, into the soft skin inside the shell, and suddenly head and legs snapped in, and the armored tail clamped in sideways."

   How it connects to theme: Anything that might threaten the turtle will be dealt with in whatever way necessary.

3. Story detail: After being hit by the truck, the turtle is flipped over and rolled off the highway. "Lying on its back, the turtle was tight in its shell for a long time. But at last its legs waved in the air, reaching for something to pull it over."

How it connects to theme: Even though the turtle runs into a temporary setback, it will do all it can to survive and keep going.

## Reading Strategy: Analyze Patterns of Symbolism, p. 208

### Sample Answers

Turtle; always looks straight ahead, plods slowly but steadily, gets knocked over by car but gets up and goes on; symbolizes human life, the will to go on even under the most adverse situation.

Oat beards, foxtails, clover burrs, etc.; catch on animals and are carried along, contain a sleeping life; symbolize the potential for reproduction and renewal.

Oat seeds; deposited on far side of road; perhaps symbolize the Joads, or people generally, moving on and beginning new life in different place with potential for growth.

## Vocabulary Builder, p. 209

**A.** 1. procrastinate
2. project
3. protrude
4. extrude

**B.** 1. raised structure
2. thrust forward
3. distribution
4. frenzied

## "Starving Peapickers" by Dorothea Lange
## "Dust Bowl Blues" by Woody Guthrie

## Primary Sources: Photographs and Ballad, p. 211
### Sample Answers

1. The woman seems on the edge of despair but still determined to go on and to do what is necessary to survive. We can infer this from the strained look on her face and the eyes that seem lifeless. She doesn't seem to have any joy left in her, but her expression doesn't suggest she is willing to give up, either.

2. Many people of that time probably had very similar experiences and responded to them in the same way by fighting on while feeling the hopelessness of an endless string of misfortunes.

3. The family is extremely poor. They have very few possessions, and these seem worn and battered.

4. You might infer that the people know how bad everything is for them, but they have not given up and can even joke about it.

5. The storms must have been overwhelming, filling the air and sky with sand and black dust, covering over fences and everything else. The wind must have been hard and constant.

## Vocabulary Builder, p. 212

**A.** 1. When the cold winds blew, the farm workers *huddled* around the fire.
2. The *migrant* workers were looking for work and a home.
3. They were *destitute*.
4. The *exposures* revealed a family struggling to survive.
5. The *agricultural* people were forced from their land.
6. None of the people were *native* to this place.

**B.** 1. B; 2. A; 3. B; 4. D

## "The Unknown Citizen" by W. H. Auden

## Literary Analysis: Satire, p. 213

Students should write a satirical slogan for each ad campaign and explain how they would present it. For example, to educate drivers about the importance of obeying traffic signs, they might suggest an image of a person being rolled on a gurney to an ambulance with the slogan, "When it said 'Stop,' it couldn't have meant *you*, Bob. After all, you were late to a party."

## Reading Strategy: Relate Structure to Meaning, p. 214

1. He worked in a factory all his life except during the war. His employers and his union were satisfied with him and he fit in well with his co-workers.

Structural Elements: The regular line lengths and rhythm create a monotonous, regular pattern that suggests the monotonous, regular pattern of his life. Capitalization of the names of certain common institutions suggests the predominant role that these institutions played in his life.

2. According to the authorities, the person fit perfectly into society's mold, purchasing all the customary consumer goods that living like everybody else requires.

Structural Elements: The use of regular rhythm and rhyme accentuates the sameness, anonymity, and predictability of life in modern society. The use of capitalization reinforces the concept that authorities tend to intrude into people's lives, prescribing how people should live.

## Vocabulary Builder, p. 215

**A.** 1. His *conduct* drew everyone's attention and his employer reminded him that he would lose his job if he continued to act in such a thoughtless manner.
2. *Psychology* is a fascinating area of research.
3. A person who is *sensible* of what he or she is doing at all times is usually a reliable friend.

**B.** 1. psychology; 2. conduct; 3. sensible

**"old age sticks"** and **"anyone lived in a pretty how town"** by E. E. Cummings

## Literary Analysis: Author's Style, p. 217

**Sample Answers**

1. Cummings's use of unconventional syntax causes the ideas to run together in unexpected ways. It's hard to tell where ideas start and stop and how they connect. The result is that Cummings forces readers to rethink their normal assumptions.
2. Cummings's unusual use of capitalization makes readers search for the beginning and ending of sentences and to reconsider how ideas are connected.
3. Cummings's minimal use of punctuation forces readers to reread lines and think carefully how ideas are related, again forcing them to reconsider their usual assumptions about these ordinary ideas.

## Reading Strategy: Paraphrase to Determine Meaning, p. 218

**Sample Answers**

Passage: "old age sticks/up Keep/Off /signs)&/youth yanks them /down. . . ."

Paraphrase: In old age, people want the young to be quiet, cautious, respectful but young people ignore the warnings.

Passage: "anyone lived in a pretty how town/with up so floating many bells down)/spring summer autumn winter/he sang his didn't' he danced his did."

Paraphrase: A man named Anyone lived in a small town where bells were always ringing. He lived there for a long time. Time passed and he lived an ordinary life.

Passage: "one day anyone died i guess/(and noone stooped to kiss his face)/busy folk buried them side by side/little by little and was by was"

Paraphrase: The man, Anyone, lived an ordinary life and in his old age died. His wife, Noone kissed him. Then Anyone was buried and when Noone died, she was buried next to him. And life went on as usual in the little town.

## Vocabulary Builder, p. 219

**A.** 1. reaped; 2. sowed
**B.** 1. C; 2. B

**"Of Modern Poetry"** by Wallace Stevens
**"Ars Poetica"** by Archibald MacLeish
**"Poetry"** by Marianne Moore

## Literary Analysis: Theme, p. 221

**Sample Answers**

1. Theme: Poetry must adjust to the people and the time to have meaning. The poet uses an image of the poem as some living thing that meets people and communicates with them. The simile that compares a poem to an actor on the stage suggests that a poem must find a way to address the audience in such a way as to be understood.
2. Theme: A poem is a living thing that must touch the human mind and spirit in many ways to have meaning. The two lines are a simile comparing a poem to a piece of fruit; that is, it is something alive that can be felt.
3. Theme: Poetry is important because it is real. Images of hands grasping and eyes dilating imply the genuineness of poetry.

## Reading Strategy: Analyze Philosophical Arguments, p. 222

Answers will vary, but students may note that all three poets share the idea that poems are concentrated, personal expressions. As imagists, all consider, and use, symbols and images to evoke intense feelings and ideas, although the feelings and ideas may vary from reader to reader. Stevens's poem expresses a view that poetry must be flexible and search for a way to communicate with its audience. MacLeish's philosophy emphasizes the living quality of poetry that allows it to touch the human spirit. Moore's philosophy is that good poetry is genuine and that it is important.

## Vocabulary Builder, p. 223

**A.** 1. He was <u>dissatisfied</u> with the quality of the food.
   2. She had an <u>insatiable</u> desire for fame.
   3. The student's incomplete report was graded <u>unsatisfactorily</u> by the teacher.
**B.** 1. palpable; 2. insatiable; 3. derivative; 4. suffice

### Contemporary Commentary

## Tim O'Brien Introduces "Ambush," p. 225

1. He means that it has a beginning, a middle, and an end; it can be understood and appreciated with no additional information.
2. The story is fiction, since the character Tim in the narrative is not identical to the author in real life, even though their names are the same.
3. Sample answers: **Factual Details:** mosquitoes, trail junction, dark night, tension, three shadowy enemy soldiers; **Fictional Details:** throwing a hand grenade, inspection of the body, gaping at the dead soldier.
4. Answers will vary. Some students will agree that O'Brien is responsible, since his participation in the violence implicates him; others will argue he is not responsible, since he cannot be sure that it was a bullet from his weapon that killed the enemy soldier.
5. The main purpose in writing the story was to express a kind of confession, or a lament. The story was the author's effort to acknowledge his responsibility for the death of a fellow human being.

## Tim O'Brien

### Listening and Viewing, p. 226

Sample answers and guidelines for evaluation:

**Segment 1:** In both fiction and magic, one must create the illusion that something is really happening even though the audience knows it is not real. Fictional books are true in an emotional and spiritual sense as they connect with human experiences, whether or not they actually happened.

**Segment 2:** The story "Ambush" includes real events, places, and names while most of the details of the story are entirely fictional. Using the word *I* gives the story a sense of authority and actuality. Students may answer that reading a story from a first-person perspective makes the story more realistic and credible.

**Segment 3:** Students may answer that revision is important because it allows them the opportunity to improve their writing. He knows that his story is finished when it "feels finished" and when the story has a harmony and sounds resolved.

**Segment 4:** Stories have the power to console, inspire, lead through tough times, and help us heal. Students may suggest that writing stories can bring out the most exciting and interesting parts of their lives and personalities.

### "In Another Country" by Ernest Hemingway

### Literary Analysis: Author's Style, p. 227

#### Sample Answers

Diction: "We all had the same medals, except the boy with the black silk bandage across his face, and he had not been at the front long enough to get any medals." The words used are simple, direct.

Tone: "The three with the medals were like hunting-hawks; and I was not a hawk, although I might seem a hawk to those who had never hunted; they, the three, knew better and so we drifted apart." Hemingway's tone is one of acceptance and is non-judgmental. He seems only to want to explain and understand his subject.

Syntax: "The major came very regularly to the hospital. I do not think he ever missed a day, although I am sure he did not believe in the machines." Although Hemingway uses some compound and complex sentences, overall the syntax is simple and direct. It's easy to follow.

### Reading Strategy: Identifying With Characters, p. 228

#### Sample Answers

1. In this passage, the major appears to be very particular about grammar. If he were the narrator, he would probably not take it so seriously and might instead ignore it altogether, being satisfied that he could understand and be understood in Italian.

2. The "hawks" looked at life differently from the narrator. Although nice men, they understood what real courage was about and knew the narrator had not displayed it. If

they were like the narrator, they might find this less important. They might remain close to the narrator simply because they found him interesting and a good companion and not give too much thought to whether he had great courage or not.

### Vocabulary Builder, p. 229

**A.** 1. disgrace, 2. detached, 3. resign

**B.** 1. The people at the café seemed to be *detached* from the sufferings of the soldiers who were defending their country.

2. The soldier tried to *resign* himself to the deaths of his comrades.

3. He forced himself to rush into combat knowing that failing to would be a *disgrace*.

### "A Rose for Emily" and "Nobel Prize Acceptance Speech" by William Faulkner

### Literary Analysis: Conflict and Resolution, p. 231

#### Sample Answers

**A.** 1. Miss Emily does not pay her taxes, and the town authorities try to bring her into compliance with the law. The conflict is external.

2. She is firm, with no emotion. She may have lost touch with reality, or she may be trying to avoid responsibility.

3. An awful smell begins to come from Miss Emily's house, and the neighbors complain. A party is organized to go in the night and sprinkle lime in her cellar and around her outbuildings.

4. The narrator appears to have a high level of respect and even awe for Miss Emily, yet he feels both pity and revulsion. Examples will vary.

5. The discovery of the body resolves what most likely caused the awful smell, why Miss Emily purchased the arsenic, and why Homer Baron was never seen again.

**B.** Students may mention that Faulkner says that the modern world is frightening, and people read to gain hope and relief from this external conflict. Students may also mention that when people have internal conflicts, they can find support or wisdom through reading.

### Reading Strategy: Clarify Ambiguities, p. 232

**A. Sample Answers**

1. B

   Supporting details: The smell is so foul that complaints are brought to the mayor. The man is eventually found dead in Miss Emily's bed.

2. C

   Supporting details: She carried her head high, demanding recognition of her dignity.

3. A

Supporting details: A Grierson would not think seriously of a Northerner, a day laborer.

**B.** Sample answer: The voices of humans are expressed in
writing that gets left behind for others to read. In this way,
humans do not die, because their message continues.

## Vocabulary Builder, p. 233

### Sample Answers

**A.** 1. N; Slaves often received *inhumane* treatment.

    2. D; The importance of eating properly is often
*ingrained.*

    3. D; He felt caught in an incoherent arguement with
his friend.

**B.** 1. The person would probably feel unhappy because the
car could not be freed from the snow.

    2. They get in trouble.

    3. Usually the more experienced team wins easily.

    4. It suggests that the person is not guilty.

    5. Doctors would tell people to get vaccinated immediately.

    6. I would ask him to respect my privacy.

## "The Jilting of Granny Weatherall"
by Katherine Anne Porter

## Literary Analysis: Stream of Consciousness, p. 235

### Sample Answers

**A.** 1. Her first sight of Doctor Harry makes her feel that
everyone is floating. When she sees him again, she
feels the presence of God but also worries about
sugar ants; then her thoughts turn to Hapsy.

    2. Granny recalls her daily routine, focusing on dusting
a clock. Thoughts of cleaning make her recall cleaning the attic and finding love letters, and that
thought leads to contemplating death itself. These
thoughts lead to a flashback to 20 years before when
she thought she was dying.

    3. Thoughts of Lydia lead Granny into a comparison of
her children; from there, her thoughts turn to John,
her long-dead husband, another flashback.

    4. Granny imagines herself being smothered by the pil-
low and that leads to a flashback about being jilted
on her wedding day.

    5. Granny's thoughts naturally turn to the state of her
soul but suddenly refocus on how John comforted
her when George jilted her, more flashbacks.

**B.** John felt he could float forever on that pillow. Look, Ma,
I can swim! I can swim! The sand was so warm, and the
water was so salty; I never wanted to go home. It was
good to feel so right about the world, but there were so
many things he'd always meant to do. Well, he'd start
doing some of these things when he came home from
the hospital.

## Reading Strategy: Clarify Sequence of Events, p. 236

### Sample Answers

1. I was pretty. I wore a Spanish comb in my hair, and I
often carried a fan.

2. We had a good, loving relationship. We worked hard and
loved our children.

3. I fenced in the fields on my own, with just a little help. I
raised the children. I rode out in all sorts of weather to
help sick people and to take care of the livestock.

4. When the children were young, I was their protector.
They looked to me to solve all their problems. Sometimes they still come to me for help. But most of the
time now, I find that I am dependent on *them.* And I
don't see them as often as I would like to.

5. When I was sixty, I became very ill. My children thought
I was going to die, but I've lived on twenty more years.
Also, I'm not afraid of death because I've made peace
with God; I think I've been a good person and lived an
honest life.

6. George was a man I was engaged to before I met John.
George jilted me on our wedding day. I've never forgotten the grief and anger I experienced on that day. The
grief and anger have stayed with me for sixty years.

## Vocabulary Builder, p. 237

**A.** 1. D; 2. C; 3. G; 4. A; 5. B; 6. F; 7. E

**B.** 1. A; 2. C; 3. D

## "A Worn Path" by Eudora Welty

## Literary Analysis: Archetype of the Hero's Quest, p. 239

### Sample Answers

**Object of journey:** to obtain medicine for grandson

**Obstacles:** long walk to town; barbed wire fence blocks way;
sees ghost; falls; shoes untied; attendant doesn't know her.

**How obstacles are overcome:** keeps walking; crawls under
fence; discovers ghost is just a scarecrow; hunter helps her
up; stranger ties shoes; nurse steps in, helps Phoenix.

**What journey symbolizes:** journey through life

## Reading Strategy: Generate Questions to Make and Confirm Predictions, p. 240

### Sample Answers

**Details:** Phoenix is frail, wild animals are all around, she's
walking in the woods.

**Prediction:** She will fall and get hurt when an animal sur-
prises her or by stumbling over rough ground.

**Details:** She is surprised by the dog and falls into a ditch.
She drifts away and dreams.

**Prediction:** The dream may become the rest of the story. She may die in the ditch.

**Details:** She sees the coin fall from the man's pocket. She distracts him. She picks up the coin.

**Prediction:** The man will realize she has tricked him and get angry.

**Details:** The attendant doesn't know Phoenix.

**Prediction:** The attendant won't give Phoenix the medicine. Phoenix will leave empty-handed.

## Vocabulary Builder, p. 241

**A.** 1. grave
2. obstinate
3. limber
4. persistent

**B.** 1. B; 2. C; 3. A; 4. D

## "The Night the Ghost Got In" by James Thurber

## Literary Analysis: Humorous Essay, p. 243

1. Idioms ("Psst!" "Awp,"); hyperbole ("despondent beagle.) The idioms make the characters seem dramatic and a little silly. The hyperbole helps readers see Herman in an absurd, picturesque light.

2. Idiom (tromping); hyperbole ("Police were all over the place," noises of the ransacking, "half-dozen policemen emerged out of the darkness). The idiom makes the description colorful and adds to the sense of exaggeration. The hyperbole makes the scene seem ridiculous with so many police about and going overboard looking for intruders, as when they look in drawers.

3. Idioms ("o'nuthin'"; "jerking a thumb at me"; "nekked"; "historical"); hyperbole (description of narrator as naked); understatement (just looked at narrator). The idioms make the cop seem not too smart and makes the narrator seem foolish. The hyperbole about the narrator being naked overstates the case since he is partly clothed. The understatement suggests a level of sarcasm.

4. Understatement (the cops' attitude toward the event); idioms ("layout," phony"). The understatement makes the reader smile because the cops probably were not just reluctant but maybe angry, confused, or some more definite opinion of the situation. The idioms highlight the ridiculousness of the situation.

## Reading Strategy: Analyzing Cause and Effect, p. 244

1. Herman wakes up with an "Awp" and wants to go back to sleep.
2. Mother throws a shoe through the neighbor's window.
3. The narrator wants to let them in, but his mother forbids him. The police have no alternative but to break down the door.
4. The policeman asks what the narrator's doing there, to which the narrator says he lives there. The policeman

then wants to know if he's hot. The narrator puts on some trousers.

5. The narrator tells him it's a zither that their guinea pig used to sleep on.
6. The police charge into the attic and Grandfather, thinking they're deserters from a battle, shoots at them, wounding one cop.
7. The narrator tells him there were ghosts. The reporter looks at him oddly and walks away.

## Vocabulary Builder, p. 245

**A.** 1. The narrator tried to *intervene* to prevent his grandfather from being descended upon by the police.
2. The man next door was sick and *despondent*.
3. The neighbor was *indignant* that someone threw a shoe through her window.
4. The narrator knew *intuitively* that it would be best not to tell his mother he had seen a ghost.

**B.** 1. intuitively
2. intervene
3. despondent
4. indignant

## "Chicago" and "Grass" by Carl Sandburg

## Literary Analysis: Personification, p. 247

**Sample Answers**

1. Clue #1: The address at the beginning of the poem: "Hog Butcher of the World," etc.; Clue #2: The use of *you* in the first section of the poem; Clue #3: The use of the imperative in the second half of the second section of the poem
2. Chicago and its critics
3. The conversation might have been a debate between Chicago and its critics.
4. Sandburg might have written a first-person account of his experiences in Chicago, or he might have written a poem that neutrally compared the good and bad points of Chicago.

## Reading Strategy: Effects of Repetition on Clarity, p. 248

**Sample Answers**

1. The repetition clarifies and emphasizes the speaker's main point: Chicago is "wicked," "crooked," "flawed." It establishes the basis for the follow-up rebuttal that comprises the rest of the poem.
2. This repetition clarifies the speaker's point that the city is hard working, dirty, and carries a terrible burden, but it laughs and is proud of it.
3. This repetition clarifies the speaker's point that soldiers keep dying in wars.
4. This repetition clarifies the speaker's point that the grass (or nature or time) covers all, no matter how terrible or ugly.

## Vocabulary Builder, p. 249

**A.** 1. C; 2. A; 3. B

**B.** 1. cunning; 2. wanton; 3. brutal; 4. brutal; 5. wanton

### Robert Frost's Poetry

## Literary Analysis: Blank Verse and Pastorals, p. 251

**A.** Students should underline syllables 2, 4, 6, 8, and 10 in each line.

**B.** Examples of the pastoral include reference to the "pathless wood," the face burning and tickling with cobwebs, and one eye weeping from being struck by a twig. The nontraditional elements include these same elements, which acknowledge that rural life is not always gentle but that it can sometimes hurt as well.

## Reading Strategy: Read Poetry in Sentences, p. 252

**A.** When I see birches bend to left and right across the lines of straighter darker trees, I like to think some boy's been swinging them.

But swinging doesn't bend them down to stay as ice storms do.

Often you must have seen them loaded with ice a sunny winter morning after a rain.

They click upon themselves as the breeze rises, and turn many colored as the stir cracks and crazes their enamel.

**B.** Number of sentences:

"Birches"—20; "Stopping By Woods on a Snowy Evening"—6; "Mending Wall"—21; "Out, Out—"—23; "The Gift Outright"—5; "Acquainted With the Night"—7

## Vocabulary Builder, p. 253

**A.** Sample Answers

1. Robert Frost remains a luminary of American poetry.
2. The luminary glow of the stars lit the path for the weary travelers.
3. The young film star's face seemed luminous through the eye of the camera.
4. Her luminosity was apparent to all her fans.
5. Robert Frost's poems illuminate a time and a place in American history.

**B.** 1. luminary; 2. rueful; 3. poise

### "The Negro Speaks of Rivers," "Dream Variations," "I, Too," and "Refugee in America"
by Langston Hughes

## Biography, p. 255

**A. Sample Answers**

**Humble Beginning:** One of the country's most successful writers. He had a difficult childhood.

**Writing and Wandering:** While going to college, Hughes formed a strong attachment to Harlem. He placed three poems beside the plate of Vachel Lindsay who declared him an important new poet.

**Renaissance Man:** Hughes helped define the spirit of the Harlem Renaissance. Besides poetry, Hughes wrote plays, fiction, musicals, autobiographies, and screenplays.

**B. Sample Answers**

1. Why did you live with your grandmother instead of your mother and then ultimately end up with your mother? I would like to know what his home life was really like so I could see more connections with his life as an adult.
2. What is the story behind your decision to place poems beside Vachel Lindsay's plate? I think it would be interesting to know what inspired him to take this action.
3. What did you find so interesting about Harlem? This city seems to have inspired Hughes as well as many other African Americans, and I think it would be interesting to know why.

## Literary Analysis: Speaker and Multiple Themes, p. 256

**Sample Answers**

**"The Negro Speaks of Rivers,"** Speaker: Black people as a race.

Clues: The time period covered is too long for a single person's lifetime. The remembrances told are part of black history.

Themes: African race is ancient; pride in African ancestry.

Clues: "I've known rivers ancient as the world"; "I bathed in the Euphrates"; "built my hut near the Congo"; "My soul has grown old like the rivers."

**"Dream Variations,"** Speaker: Black person who takes great pride in his or her race.

Clues: Written in first person. Clues like "Dark like me" and "Black like me" identify speaker as black.

Themes: African Americans cannot yet enjoy all the privileges of the white world, but the speaker dreams of the time when black people will have all those rights.

Clues: "Till the white day is done"; "While night comes on gently,/Dark like me—"

**"I, Too"** Speaker: Black man experiencing discrimination.

Clues: Written in first person. Speaker says people like him are Americans and should have same rights as others.

Themes: African Americans are an equal part of American society; past discrimination; confidence in future of freedom

Clues: "I, too, sing America"; "I'll be at the table/When company comes."

**"Refugee in America"** Speaker: Probably an ex-slave.

Clues: Written in first person. Speaker knows worth of freedom and almost makes speaker cry.

Themes: African Americans long for freedom and liberty, experiences they do not yet enjoy fully.

Clues: "words like *Freedom*/Sweet and wonderful to say"; "*Liberty*/That almost make me cry."

## Reading Strategy: Applying Critical Perspectives, p. 257

1. A historical perspective helps readers recognize the clues that suggest the speaker might be a former slave, someone who "had known what I knew" about liberty and freedom.

2. The speaker is writing from the perspective of the entire black race, one whose history spans time from the distant past to the present.

3. A social and historical perspective helps readers understand that African Americans have long been denied equal access to the dinner table, as well as to many other aspects of American life.

4. A social perspective helps readers understand why contemporary African Americans might lament the "white day" in which they can only dream of playing in and long for night when the dark color of the African American skin is not a limitation to enjoying life fully.

## Vocabulary Builder, p. 258

**A.** 1. liberalize; 2. liberal arts; 3. liberally; 4. libertarian

**B.** 1. D; 2. B; 3. A

## Grammar and Style: Pronoun-Antecedent Agreement, p. 259

**A.** 1. his or her
2. her
3. its
4. his
5. their

**B.** 1. Most readers have their favorite poems by Langston Hughes.
2. Correct
3. Each of the poets in this anthology has his or her own perspectives on life and society.
4. Correct
5. The poem about rivers was interesting because it creates images of many times and places.

## "Study the Masters" by Lucille Clifton

## "For My Children" by Colleen McElroy

## Literary Analysis: Poetry of Cultural Identity, p. 261

**Sample Answers**

**"Study the Masters"**

Roots: "like my aunt timmie./it was her iron"; "some masai"

Cultural knowledge: "if you had heard her/chanting as she ironed/you would understand form and line/and discipline and order and/America"

Language: "she dreamed too, words: some Cherokee, some masai,"

Art forms: "the master poet" "chanting as she ironed"

**"For My Children":**

Roots: "I search for a heritage beyond St. Louis"; "Watusi shadows"

Cultural knowledge: "effigies of my ancestors are captured / In Beatle tunes" "While I cling to one stray Seminole."

Language: "skin of honey and beauty of ebony," "calabash," "Dahomey"

Art forms: "Beatle tunes," "totem of the Burundi"

## Vocabulary Builder, p. 262

**A.** 1. The *effigies* of a Bantu chief and a Watusi warrior stood upon the shelf, two reminders of her African heritage.
2. She sat quietly, waiting for the *rituals* to begin.
3. The blanket represented beautiful *handiwork* that had been passed down for generations.

**Sample Answers**

**B.** 1. The ancient rituals were powerful reminders of their African heritage.
2. The effigies were placed around the room where each could be seen one at a time.
3. Many examples of her handiwork could be seen throughout the house.

## Poems by Claude McKay, Countee Cullen, and Arna Bontemps

## Literary Analysis: Stanza Structure, p. 264

**Sample Answers**

1. 3 stanzas
2. Stanza 1: There are many wonderful fruits fit for a prize.
   Stanza 2: The fruit bring back memories of fruit in another place.
   Stanza 3: The memories make the speaker long for the place in his memory.
3. sonnet
4. Stanza 1: We shall not always serve others.
   Stanza 2: We have strong qualities of our own. In the meantime, we are sad, but we await the time when we can blossom.
5. 3 stanzas
6. Stanza 1: I have worked hard planting and worried about losing it.
   Stanza 2: Although I have planted much, I have only reaped enough to fill my hand.
   Stanza 3: My work has gone to support others who have not worked and my children are bitter because of it.

## Reading Strategy: Apply a Political Approach to Literary Criticism, p. 265

1. Answers will vary. Most students will say this poem is not strongly related to political events so knowing the political climate of this period is not especially helpful.

2. The political reality of the 1920s found African Americans living generally as second-class citizens. A great many worked in service jobs caring for white people. Many African Americans no doubt hid "the heart that bleeds" and waited for change.

3. As with "From the Dark Tower," "A Black Man Talks of Reaping" refers directly to the political realities of the African American experience during and before the mid-twentieth century when African Americans were forced to work in menial jobs. Most of the fruits of their labors went to people who did not work while they struggled to survive. Awareness of this situation was a "bitter fruit."

## Vocabulary Builder, p. 266

**A.** 1. D
   2. A
   3. C
   4. C
**B.** 1. C; 2. B; 3. D; 4. A

## from Dust Tracks on a Road
by Zora Neale Hurston

### Literary Analysis: Social Context in Autobiography, p. 268

1. She reveals that her family functioned in a completely segregated world, where they often lived in fear of the actions of white people. The forwardness she shows in offering to walk a while with the white folks frightens her family.

2. She reveals that her community was made up of people like herself. To Hurston, the homogeneity of the village was isolated and boring.

3. Hurston reveals here that her school was a spectacle for whites—they were intrigued by an all-black school and watched the proceedings much like they would have watched a show or performance.

Student responses about their own social context will vary. Generally, students can make a connection to feelings of isolation, awkwardness, and boredom.

### Reading Strategy: Analyzing Author's Purpose and Its Impact on Meaning, p. 269

**Sample Responses**

1. This event shows that Hurston hasn't really had much experience with white people, especially sophisticated ones. It helps the reader see how separated she was from white people, perhaps because her community was totally African American.

2. The white ladies' request may show that they don't trust her abilities, thinking perhaps the reading she did in school was memorized. Hurston may want the reader to see that although well-intentioned, these women refused to take her fluent reading at face value because it contradicted their stereotypes about African Americans.

3. Her thoughts about these characters show that Hurston has a strong moral bent and admires people who take action rather than talking about things. She chooses these details to reveal aspects of her character.

4. Hurston rides about half a mile with the white travelers and walks back. This shows that she is bored with Orlando and gives the reader the idea that she will get out of Orlando as soon as she can.

5. Hurston's purpose in much of the selection is to reveal how little white people and African Americans knew about each other. By recognizing this purpose, it encourages readers to look for these details and to gain greater insight into their meaning.

## Vocabulary Builder, p. 270

**A.** 1. B; 2. D; 3. C; 4. A
**B.** 1. F. People who act with brazenness usually have a great deal of confidence because it takes confidence to act shamelessly and with boldness.

   2. T. An hour is long enough to both eat lunch and visit with friends.

   3. F. Students almost always feel badly when they do poorly on an examination.

   4. T. Usually, when people plan a prank, they expect to have fun with it.

# Unit 5

## Names and Terms to Know Worksheet, p. 273

**A. (Possible answers)**

1. The Cold War is the basically bloodless conflict of wills between the U.S. and Soviet Union after World War II

2. The Silent Generation are those who came of age in the conformist 1950s.

3. Sputnik was the world's first artificial satellite launched into space by the Soviet Union.

4. *The Crucible* is Arthur's Miller's play about the McCarthy hearings, but set during the Salem witch hunts centuries earlier

5. John Hersey was an American author who wrote *Hiroshima.*

6. Martin Luther King, Jr. spearheaded the Civil Rights movement as it took shape in the South in the 1950s.

**B. (Possible responses)**

1. The 1950s prized normality and conformity; the 1960s celebrated disorder and individuality. The 1950s quietly suffered anxiety over the Atomic Age. The 1960s protested noisily against authority or escaped it through drugs and popular culture.

2. Suburban life encouraged both conformity and isolation. The suburbs thrived as people prospered in the 1950s and left the cities for homes with yards. The suburbs replaced the small town.

3. The Civil Rights movement desegregated schools and other facilities in the South and made Americans more

aware of the need for racial equality. It helped African Americans gain more opportunities.

## Essential Question Worksheet, p. 274

**A. (Possible responses)**

1. a. The Cold War and nuclear arms race between the U.S. and Soviet Union made Americans anxious. In the 1960s, American involvement in Vietnam's civil war divided the country.

   b. the Civil Rights movement and Women's Movement

2. a. The Age of Anxiety represented a reaction to the horrors of World War II and the horrors of living under the threat of nuclear war. People during this time valued material prosperity and conformity.

   b. The Age of Aquarius was the late 1960s, when the orderliness of the 1950s gave way to protest for social justice and resistance against living with fear and conformity. It valued individualism and freedom.

3. a. Joseph Heller and Kurt Vonnegut

   b. Writers wrote to promote racial equality and expose injustice. In general, writers protested against conformity and the ills of postwar society.

   c. Broadway musical comedies, telvision shows, popular music like that of the Beatles

**B. (Possible responses)**

1. exploring new experiences and made her a little dull

2. take up yoga

3. it makes them believe that good is possible

## Essential Question Worksheet p. 275

**A. (Possible responses)**

1. a. They made Americans wonder if the dream was enough and worth the price of struggling for succcess.

   b. In the American Revolution, people rebelled against another power, from overseas. During the 1960s rebellion, Americans protested against their own society and culture.

   c. White Americans became aware of the need for racial equity when they heard the speeches of Martin Luther King, Jr.

2. a. Writers witnessed the horrors of war, as well as the current state of American society.

   b. Writers withdrew from mainstream society, rebelling against it, supporting causes aimed at changing society. They broke with artistic and social norms.

   c. Some writers spoke for the masses who participated in social movements, particularly the Civil Rights movement and Women's movement.

3. a. Arthur Miller used the Salem witch trials to criticize "witch hunts" for possible and former Communists in American society.

   b. Lowell, Bishop, and Wilbur wrote in traditional forms such as sonnets and sestinas, but expressed modern views in these forms. Steinbeck continued to write realistic fiction, and the Southern Gothic traidtion continued in the work of Faulkner, McCullers, and O'Connor.

c. Williams, Stevens, and Hemingway continued to develop the Modernist style.

**B. (Possible responses)**

1. travel to Europe for the family vacation for the first time.

2. learn a new language.

3. his lack of interest in their latest project: robots.

## Essential Question Worksheet, p. 276

**A. (Possible responses)**

1. a. Randall Jarrell, Norman Mailer, John Hersey, among others

   b. Writing after World War I, though filled with pain, shows the possibility of heroism and courage, as opposed to the sense of waste after World War I.

2. a. the works of Bellow, Roth, Salinger, Malamud, Miller, and Hansberry.

   b. The image of the city appeared in many poems as a symbol of modern American life.

3. a. a chance to make the American dream more accessible

   b. Some American writers—John Updike and John Cheever— saw the suburbs as isolating and empty

   c. Many American writers associated the American Dream with stifling conformity.

**B. (Possible responses)**

1. we talk about politics

2. an organized movement to preserve other landmark buildings

3. because suburban houses are relatively close together and suburbs have malls.

## Follow-Through Activities, p. 277

### A. Check Your Comprehension

Guidelines: Students should complete the chart with other concepts appropriate to the period and the groups that are associated with these concepts.

### B. Extend Your Learning

Guidelines: Students should complete the chart with answers that will help them to do their research.

## Literary Analysis: Implied Theme, p. 278

1. a. objective—uses third-person point of view to report factually on the events experienced by Mr. Tanimoto; b. This excerpt shows how war disrupts the lives of its victims. It also emphasizes the feelings and humanity of people seen only as "the enemy" or as casualties of war.

2. a. objective—uses third-person point of view to report factually on the catastrophic effect of the atomic blast on the tin factory; b. This excerpt shows the destructive nature of war and how human knowledge, as represented by the books, can be destructive. Human knowledge is responsible for creating the terrifying weapon of mass destruction.

3. a. subjective—the poet uses poetic language ("loosed from its dream of life") and first-person narration to convey the subjective emotional experience of the ball turret

gunner's reactions to being under enemy attack; b. This excerpt reveals the cruel and frightening nature of war through the eyes of a gunner perched below a World War II bomber. It emphasizes how death during war is treated with indifference—as if the soldiers fighting are merely killing machines.

4. This excerpt reveals the cruel and frightening nature of war through the eyes of a gunner perched below a World War II bomber. It emphasizes how death during war is treated with indifference—as if the soldiers fighting are merely killing machines.

## Reading Strategy: Analyze Political Assumptions, p. 279

### Suggested Responses

**from *Hiroshima*—details:** Students' should include information such as Hersey's specific details, the ordinary day-to-day activities of the people, flashbacks, the settings of people's daily routines, the air raid warnings, and so forth; assumptions: students should note that Hersey's examples all point to the horrifying, destructive impact of war, especially on civilians, and that such details shows that Hersey is opposed to war in general and probably does not feel that the military advantages of dropping the bomb on Hiroshima was worth the price in innocent human suffering.

**"The Death of the Ball Turret Gunner"—details:** "from mother's sleep I fell into the State"—a fall from innocence and love into impersonal terror; "hunched in its belly till my wet fur froze"—picture of animal-like terror; "black flak and nightmare fighters"—the horror of facing death in battle; "they washed me out of the turret with a hose"—the impersonal nature of warfare; assumptions: war—any war—is an impersonal, hellish, terrifying nightmare with no redeeming qualities

## Vocabulary Builder, p.280

A. 1. barricade
   2. reconnaissance
   3. khaki
   4. blitz
   5. coup

B. 1. A; 2. C; 3. A; 4. D; 5. B; 6. C

## Editorial: "Backing the Attack"
## Editorial Cartoon: "The Battle of the Easy Chair"

## Advertisement Poster: "Junk Rally"
## Primary Sources Worksheet, p. 282

### Sample Answers
### Thesis

Editorial: The war is very costly, but if everyone buys war bonds, we can pay for it.

Editorial Cartoon: This is no time to be complacent—everyone must be actively involved in the war effort.

Poster: Junk metal is a valuable commodity that can be used to make weapons and other equipment.

### Facts and Figures

Editorial: The editorial uses many facts and figures related to the cost of the war.

Editorial Cartoon: No facts and figures—just a suggestion that the war will not be won quickly

Poster: Facts related to the upcoming junk rally, such as time, place, and purpose

### Visual Elements

Editorial: None, except for different type faces to set off newspaper title and the quotation by Roosevelt

Editorial Cartoon: The entire cartoon is a visual element.

Poster: Includes visual elements of illustrations, boxed text, and varying type faces

### Humor

Editorial: No humor

Editorial Cartoon: Humorous depiction of complacent gentleman

Poster: Humor in the visual of the iron hitting the man in the head

### Quotations

Editorial: Quotation by Roosevelt

Editorial Cartoon: No quotations

Poster: No quotations

### Catchy phrases

Editorial: No catchy phrases

Editorial Cartoon: The buttons on the gentleman's suit jacket have catchy phrases.

Poster: "Let's Jolt them with Junk from Winchester."

### Appeal to Emotion

Editorial: Mentioning that small bond purchases would "outfit a sailor" or "buy a parachute"

Editorial Cartoon: The valet's worried look

Poster: Suggesting that donating scrap metal helps the war effort

### Appeal to Logic

Editorial: Presenting the costs of the war as inducement to buy war bonds

Editorial Cartoon: None. This is an emotional appeal.

Poster: More emotional than logical

## Vocabulary Builder, p. 283

### A. Sample Answers

1. Yes, it is likely that you offended someone with your loose and inappropriate behavior.

2. No, a lazy person would avoid any serious task or challenge because it would take too much effort.

3. A team of five would do a better job of canvassing a neighborhood because they could talk to more people in a shorter amount of time than one person could.

4. A collective sigh by one hundred people would take about the same amount of time as the sigh of one person because they'd all be sighing together.

5. My weekly expenditures include lunch money, bus fare, and video rentals.

6. Estimates are not accurate predictions of what a house would sell for; they just give a general idea.

7. A company's receipts represent its income.

8. A civilian is not likely to be wearing a military uniform (unless it's for a costume party) because a civilian does not belong to the military.

9. A fire department might call on its auxiliary firefighters when it needs help putting out a fire.

10. Examples of salvage people can recover include sunken ships, old cars, old appliances, used tires, and used bricks.

## B. Sample responses

1. The new manager hoped to decrease expenditures by purchasing less paper.

2. The town required the collective effort of the community to build the new library.

3. Estimates claim that approximately 17,000 people attended the free concert last night.

### "The Life You Save May Be Your Own" by Flannery O' Connor

## Literary Analysis: Grotesque Characters, p. 284

### Sample Responses

1. The woman is obsessed with her daughter and thinks the girl is a valuable prize. She would do anything to assure that her daughter is never parted from her.

2. Mr. Shiftlet is obsessed with the idea that cars are too expensive and that no pride of workmanship goes into them. Because of this obsession, he can be expected to be proud of any car he might have; he would take good care of it.

3. Mr. Shiftlet thinks the rest of the world is rotten, and he fails to see the rottenness in himself. A man like Mr. Shiftlet is likely to take advantage of other people, thinking he deserves any advantage he can get.

## Reading Strategy: Draw Conclusion from Details, p. 285

### Sample Responses

1. The man will turn out to be someone to fear.

2. She will convince Mr. Shiftlet to marry her daughter.

3. They will / will not get married.

4. Mr. Shiftlet is going to get money out of Mrs. Crater, though he wants it for other purposes than Lucynell.

5. Mr. Shiftlet is uncomfortable with the marriage and may take action to end it.

6. He is leaving Lucynell to move on by himself.

## Vocabulary Builder, p. 286

### A. Sample Responses

1. Mr. Shiftlet was a solitary figure as he made his way toward the house.

2. After their departure, Mrs. Crater was the sole occupant of the farm.

3. Mrs. Crater was solely responsible for Lucynell.

4. Mrs. Crater and Lucynell lived in solitude on their isolated farm.

### B. Sample Responses

1. The shed listed as if it were perched on a hill, even though the ground was perfectly flat.

2. His manner of guffawing never failed to draw attention from passersby.

3. The desolate setting could do nothing but cause despair in the characters and in the readers.

4. Her disappointment caused her to be morose for days until she regained her spirits.

5. The ravenous children kept coming back for more helpings of stew.

6. The dark clouds in the distance were an ominous sight.

### "The First Seven Years" by Bernard Malamud

## Literary Analysis: Epiphany, p. 288

### Sample Responses

1. Not epiphany—Feld is remembering something that he has thought before.

2. Not epiphany—The wish is not a moment of insight that reveals something significant about life.

3. Not epiphany—Feld merely decides on an alternative plan of action.

4. Not epiphany—Feld has learned about something that is going on. He has a heart attack but no profound insights.

5. Epiphany—Feld suddenly understands that Sobel and Miriam have been cultivating a close relationship over the past five years. There has been much more going on between his daughter and his assistant than he had ever imagined.

## Reading Strategy: Summarizing, p. 289

Sample responses: Miriam—relationship: Feld loves Miriam but does not understand her; learns: He sees that she will never marry Max but is in love with Sobel; Sobel—relationship: Feld admires Sobel as a worker but looks down on him as a person because he does not understand his love of books and ideas; learns: he realizes that because Sobel and Miriam share deep personal values, they will eventually marry. Max—relationship: Feld admires Max as an ambitious young man with a solid future; learns: Feld realizes that Max and Miriam have nothing in common and will not make a good match.

## Vocabulary Builder, p. 290

**A. Sample Responses**

1. literate—able to read, or knowledgeable about written works
2. literature—written work; writings; printed matter

**B. Sample Responses**

1. Feld thinks Max has *diligence* because he sees him going to school every day. Miriam has chosen not to go to school.
2. They are *not illiterate* because they can both read.
3. An *unscrupulous* employee might steal, do poor work, or lie.
4. Feld felt he could *discern* qualities in Max that Miriam could not perceive.
5. It was a poor, rough place, and Feld did not want Miriam to be exposed to such things; the idea was *repugnant*.

## "Constantly Risking Absurdity" by Lawrence Ferlinghetti

## Literary Analysis: Extended Metaphor, p. 292

### Sample Responses

**Possible responses:** "Constantly risking absurdity / and death"—taking great creative risks with language and meaning; "climbs on a high wire of his own making"—sets high standards and goals to be achieved in the art of poetry; "performing entrechats / and sleight of foot tricks"—takes bold leaps of the imagination and makes agile and subtle use of words; "And he / little charleychaplin man"—the poet is really a poor hapless soul in the face of his grand ambitions; "who may or may not catch / her eternal fair form"—there are no guarantees that the poet will achieve his/her goal of capturing beauty and truth in words.

## Reading Strategy: Visualize or Picture the Action, p. 293

### Possible Responses

1. In picturing that image, I think about the high standards and ambitions that the poet sets for him/herself.
2. I visualize both great physical power of the kind needed to perform leaps such as entrechats and the very fine finesse skills needed to perform fancy footwork ("sleight-of-foot tricks"); these skills translate into the poet's work as the ability to write poems that take bold leaps of the imagination and make very nimble and fine use of words.
3. I picture a mass of people who are hungry for amazement and spectacle—in the case of poetry, to be amazed by the spectacle of truth and beauty as created by the poet's words.
4. I visualize a modest, hapless, nervous person who is afraid of his own shadow. Students' responses will vary, depending on how much they know about or have seen of Charley Chaplin's films. Accept any response that seems well grounded in the language of the image.

## Vocabulary Builder, p. 294

**A. Sample Responses**

1. No, she was not agreeing, because absurdity means "senselessness" or "silliness."
2. Yes, she was paying the movie a compliment, because taut means "tight" or "tense," which means that it was a well-plotted movie.
3. No, his program would not contain any unreasonable demands because *realist* means "one who is practical or unidealistic."

**B.** 1. b; 2. c; 3. a

## "Mirror" by Sylvia Plath
## "Courage" by Anna Sexton

## Literary Analysis: Figurative Language, p. 296

### Sample Response:

Students might identify four of the following or any others they identify—accept any reasonable interpretation of the figures of speech: "The eye of a little god, four-cornered"—metaphor—the mirror has the truth-telling powers of a god; "Now I am a lake"—metaphor—the mirror reflects its surroundings as faithfully as a lake; " . . . and in me an old woman / Rises toward her day after day, like a terrible fish"—simile—the sight of her aging face is like a terrible monster from the deep; "the child's first step, as awesome as an earthquake"—simile—the child's first step is a momentous event; "Your courage was a small coal / that you kept swallowing"—metaphor—your courage was a difficult but necessary feat of survival; "love as simple as shaving soap"—simile—love is a simple, homespun, direct feeling; "each spring will be a sword you'll sharpen"—metaphor—in old age, each passing year will arm you with deeper wisdom and courage.

## Reading Strategy: Interpreting the Connotations of Words, p. 297

### Sample Responses

1. The mirror, as narrator of the poem, views itself as an infallible reflection of the world around it; as the poem progresses, we see that the all-powerful mirror seems threatening to the woman who sees in it her progress into old age—so the mirror can be said to "swallow" everything that looks into it because it devours any illusions that people might have as they look into it.
2. The mirror regards itself as an objective, almost merciless recorder of the world that surrounds it. So anything that would tend to hide certain visual realities in soft light—like candles or the moon—are not giving the full truth of what is to be seen and are therefore "liars" by the mirror's standards of cold, honest, total reflection of reality.
3. The poet states that despair can be a transfusion—something that gives you added strength—in the belief that we learn from suffering and that it can therefore make us wiser and stronger. Therefore, through the use

of the word transfusion, the poet drives home the point that if we endure and overcome despair, then despair can strengthen us rather than weaken us.

4. In this passage, the word *banner* connotes glory or pride. The use of the word emphasizes that the soldier acted courageously not for glory or ego but out of duty and conscience—so the courage is more noble because it aims to help others rather than to enhance one's own sense of grandeur or importance.

## Vocabulary Builder, p. 298

**Possible responses:**

1. No, she would not think that you approached your topic with an open mind, because *preconceptions* means "ideas formed beforehand."

2. Yes, it is likely that he gave it an unfavorable review because *endured* means "held up under; withstood."

3. No, you would not be donating the blood, because *transfusion* means "the transferring of a live-giving substance from a source to a recipient," so you would be receiving the blood.

4. Yes, the movie had a powerful effect on her, because *transformed* means "altered; changed."

**B.** 1. A; 2. A; 3. C; 4. B;

## "Cuttings" and "Cuttings *later*" by Theodore Roethke

## Literary Analysis: Sound Devices, p. 300

**Sample Response**

1. This urge, wrestle, resurrection of dry sticks, . . .; alliteration—emphasizes the struggle to generate new life.

2. What saint strained so much, . . . ; alliteration and assonance—emphasizes the struggle and difficulty involved in generating new life.

3. I can hear, underground, that sucking and sobbing. . . .; alliteration—emphasizes the turbulent, emotionally wrenching process of generation and birth; also consonance, in the final *ng* consonant sound of *sucking* and *sobbing*.

4. When sprouts break out, . . . ; assonance—emphasizes the sudden, startling quality of the emergence of the sprouts; also consonance—the *t* sounds in *sprouts* and *out.*

## Reading Strategy: Using Background Knowledge, p. 301

**Sample Responses**

1. Roethke's grandparents immigrated from Germany and settled in Saginaw, Michigan, where they made a living growing and selling plants.

2. Roethke's father and uncle went into the plant business, which they inherited from their parents. They did very well in the business, ending up with one of the largest commercial greenhouses in the state.

3. Roethke spent countless hours of his childhood in the greenhouse, where he learned a good deal about the art and science of gardening, especially making new plants from cuttings.

4. A cutting—also known as a slip—is a twig, branch, or leaf cut from a mature plant and placed in water or wet sand.

5. Diffusion occurs when water molecules move from areas of high concentration to areas of low concentration by passing through the walls of cells.

6. As more and more water enters the cells of the cutting, water pressure builds, which in turn causes the cutting to stand upright. Water pressures also stimulates cell growth, and soon, under the proper conditions, the cutting will sprout new roots and leaves.

## Vocabulary Builder, p. 302

**Possible responses:**

**A.** 1. No, the solution was not a simple one, because *intricate* means "complex."

2. No, the water was not leaking quickly, because *seeping* means "flowing slowly."

3. Yes, the movie was scary, because *quail* means "draw back in fear."

**B.** 1. C; 2. D; 3. B;

## "The Explorer" by Gwendolyn Brooks "Frederick Douglass" by Robert Hayden

## Literary Analysis: Repetition and Parallelism, p. 304

**Possible responses:**

**"The Explorer"**

1. "Wee griefs, grand griefs"—both;

2. "There were no bourns. / There were no quiet rooms"—emphasize a message.

**"Frederick Douglass"**

1. "this beautiful / and terrible thing . . . / the beautiful, needful thing"—both

2. "when it is finally won; when it is more than the gaudy mumbo jumbo . . ."—emphasize a message.

## Reading Strategy: Read the Poems Aloud, p. 305

**Sample Responses**

Students should choose any passage of the poem that is especially meaningful to them. In each case, students should identify the main technique in evidence in the passage—parallelism, repetition, or both—and then briefly summarize how reading the passage aloud enhanced the meaning of the poem for them. Sample responses:

**"The Explorer"**

Passage: "Somehow to find a still spot in the noise/ Was the frayed inner want, the winding, the frayed hope. . . ."; technique: repetition, parallelism; enhanced meaning: emphasizes the explorer's confusion and desperation.

**"Frederick Douglass"**

Passage: "visioning a world where none is lonely, none hunted, alien . . ."; technique: parallelism; enhanced meaning: reinforces nobility and splendor of Douglass's idealistic vision of life.

## Vocabulary Builder, p. 306

**Possible responses:**

**A.** 1. a. physically worn or degraded; b. emotionally worn down or tested
   2. a. showy or cheap in decor; b. pretentious in attitude.

**B.** 1. C; 2. A; 3. C

## "One Art" and "The Filling Station"
### by Elizabeth Bishop

## Literary Analysis: Diction, p. 308

Students might mention six of the following or other details from the poem: "dirty, oil-soaked monkey suit"; "greasy sons"; "cement porch"; "set of crushed and grease-impregnated wickerwork"; "a dirty dog, quite comfy"; "comic books provide the only note of color:; "big dim doily"; "taboret"; "big hirsute begonia"; "daisy stitch with marguerites"; "gray crochet"; "cans . . . that softly say: ESSO—SO—SO—SO."

## Reading Strategy: Read According to Punctuation, p. 309

1. The exclamation point causes the reader to pause longer and to give greater emphasis to the line, which communicates the speaker's first and strongest overall impression of the filling station.
2. These lines from "The Filling Station" express two sentences or complete ideas.
3. Commas indicate pauses, not full stops, so it is not a reasonable conclusion. Not every line in this stanza expresses a complete thought. The comma after "vaster" in the first line is merely a pause in a thought that ends with the period after "continent."
4. The fourth stanza of "One Art" expresses the most complete thoughts It contains four sentences, and hence four complete thoughts.

## Vocabulary Builder, p. 310

**A. Possible responses**

1. extraterrestrial—beyond the confines of the worth
2. extrapolate—to go outside or beyond known data or knowledge to make an inference
3. extralegal—outside of or beyond the law or legality
4. extramarital—outside of marriage

**B.** 1. A; 2. A; 3. C; 4.B

## "The Rockpile" by James Baldwin

## Literary Analysis: Setting, p. 312

**A.** 1. B; 2. E; 3. C, E; 4. D, E; 5. E, G

**B.** 1. At the end of the street nearest their house was the bridge that spanned the San Francisco Bay.
   2. John and Roy sat on the veranda and watched the busy street below.
   3. Dozens of boys fought each other in the blinding blizzard.
   4. One Tuesday, an hour after his father came home, Roy was wounded on the mountain and brought screaming inside.
   5. They filled the air, too, with flying streamers, confetti, roses, hats, whatever could be picked up and thrown.

## Reading Strategy: Identify Cause and Effect, p. 313

**Possible Responses**

1. EFFECT: Roy is spoiled.
   EFFECT: Elizabeth resents Gabriel.
2. CAUSE: Gabriel intimidates John.
   CAUSE: Elizabeth speaks for John.
3. EFFECT = CAUSE: Gabriel discovers Roy's injury.
   EFFECT = CAUSE: Gabriel blames John and Elizabeth.
   EFFECT = CAUSE: Elizabeth stands up to Gabriel.

## Vocabulary Builder, p. 314

**A.** 1. Superior
   2. supercilious
   3. supersede
   4. supervisor

**B.** 1. B; 2. D; 3. C; 4. B; 5. C;

## Grammar and Style: Avoiding Shifts in Verb Tense, p. 315

**Sample Responses:**

1. I will write a thank-you note to all the guests when I get home.
2. There were lots of exciting music acts at the concert I attended.
3. It is the duty of all citizens to help all those who are in need.
4. Last year's basketball team had a losing record despite the high hopes we had for it.
5. correct

## "Life in His Language" by Toni Morrison

## Literary Analysis: Eulogy and Mood, p. 317

**Sample Responses**

Students should recognize the basic mood of "On James Baldwin as celebratory, proud, and/or loving. They might cite examples from among the following or cite additional examples not listed here: "Well, the season was always Christmas with you there. . . ."; "You gave me a language to

dwell in, a gift so perfect it seems my own invention. . . .";
"You made American English honest. . . ."; "you gave us
undecorated truth"; "Yours was the courage to live life in
and from its belly. . . ."; "Yours was a tenderness, a vulnerability, that asked everything, expected anything. . . ."; "This,
then is no calamity. No. This is jubilee."

## Reading Strategy: Analyze Syntax and Patterns of Organization, p. 318

1. Gift: "You gave me a language to dwell in, a gift so perfect it seems my own invention"; significance: Baldwin
   reshaped literary language to make it more honest and
   direct, more responsive to the feelings and concerns of
   African American readers and writers.
2. Gift: "The second gift was your courage. . . ."; significance: The courage that Baldwin showed in a variety of
   ways—moral, intellectual, political, artistic—set an
   example for an emerging generation of African American
   activists and writers who were struggling to find an
   identify and voice in a white-dominated society.
3. Gift: "your tenderness . . ."; significance: Baldwin's
   tenderness and generosity enabled him to share his
   gifts and insights with others in a way that inspired
   them to strive to be better people and artists.

## Vocabulary Builder, p. 319

**A.**
1. False—the summation will come at the end of the
   lawyer's remarks, because *summation* means "sum-
   ming up."
2. True—the executive will need to know about the con-
   sequences of every conceivable scenario, which
   means "situation."
3. True—an original essay will not rely on platitudes,
   which are "tired expressions."
4. False—The writer who appropriates from other
   authors is not careful about citing his sources,
   because appropriate means "to take or use something without permission."

**B.** 1. D; 2. A; 3. D; 4. D

## "Inaugural Address" by John F. Kennedy
### *from* "Letter from Birmingham City Jail" by Martin Luther King, Jr.

## Literary Analysis: Persuasion, p. 321

Students responses might include the following examples:
Kennedy—parallel structure: "symbolizing and end, as well
as a beginning—signifiying renewal, as well as change"—the
parallel structure helps to persuade the reader of the significance of the occasion of his inauguration.
King: 'if you would observe their ugly and inhuman treatment . . .; if you would watch them push and curse . . .; if
you would see the slap . . ."—the parallel structure helps to
persuade the reader of the repeated instances of police
brutality.

Antithesis: "the belief that the rights of man come not from
the generosity of the state, but from the hand of God"—the
antithesis drives home the contrast between the American
view of rights as derived from God's merciful spirit as
opposed to the communist doctrine in which the state is the
source of all moral authority.
Kennedy—Anaphora: "Nor will it be finished in the first 1,000
days, nor in the life of this Administration, nor perhaps even
in our lifetime on this planet"—the anaphora, by successively
extending the time in which the task might be accomplished,
persuades the reader of its magnitude and importance.
King: "Before the Pilgrims landed at Plymouth were here.
Before the pen of Jefferson etched across the pages o history
the majestic words of the Declaration of Independence, we
were here"—the anaphora helps to persuade the reader of
King's assertion that African Americans have been part of
North America's history for as long as—or longer than—any
other group.

## Reading Strategy: Identify Main Idea and Supporting Details, p. 322

Type of document—Kennedy: speech; King: Letter.
Audience: Kennedy: world and national public; King: world
and national public. Purpose—Kennedy: to inspire and lead;
King: to arouse moral conscience and action.  Example of
Argument—Kennedy: "To those old allies . . . at odds and
split asunder" (emphasizes the importance of unity among
allies); King: "So I have tried to make it clear that it is wrong
to use immoral means to attain moral ends" (argues that the
restraint of the police is in the service of immoral segregation). Example of List—Kennedy: "Let both sides . . . etc.";
King: "If you would . . . . if you would . . . etc."

## Vocabulary Builder, p. 323

**A.** 1. averted
   2. diverting
   3. vertically
   4. vertigo
   5. convert

**B.** Sample Responses
   1. They would want to join forces against their enemies.
   2. The country might disputed border the other coun-
      try's border claims, might have a disagreement about
      trade policy, or might have a history of ethnic conflict
      with the other country.
   3. You might want to get rid of a stain.
   4. He or she could invite a friend over to play a game.
   5. He or she might not be used to a verbal attack.
   6. Segregation went boldly against what was the
      nation's law.

## Grammar and Style: Use Active, Not Passive, Voice, p. 324

**A.** 1. When the influence of Gandhi's philosophy on King
   *was posed* (P) by the questioner, the professor

*affirmed* (A) that King *considered* (A) himself a disciple of Gandhi's philosophy of nonviolence.

2. Many presidents *have delivered* (A) forgettable or undistinguished inaugural addresses; Kennedy's address, by contrast, *is considered* (P) among the finest and most memorable by many historians.

3. *Ask* (A) not what your country *can do* (A) for you.

4. . . . we *were carrying* (A) our whole nation back to those great wells of democracy which *were dug* deep (P) by the Founding Fathers. . .

## B. Possible responses

1. We will not finish all this in the first 100 days.

2. History has granted only a few generations the role of defending freedom in its hour of maximum danger.

3. Let us hope that that we can lift the deep fog of misunderstanding from our fear-drenched communities.

4. Many communities throughout the country have honored Dr. Martin Luther King, Jr., by naming schools and streets after him.

## *from* the Author's Desk

### The Words of Arthur Miller on The Crucible, p. 326

1. The "correspondence" was between the Salem witch trials of 1692 and the anticommunist campaigns in American politics during the late 1940s and early 1950s.

2. He says that there must have been something marvelous in the spectacle of an entire village whose imagination was captured by a vision of something that didn't exist.

3. In both cases, the prosecutions alleged membership in a secret, disloyal group; in both cases, the honesty of a confession could be proved only by the willingness of the accused to name former confederates or associates.

4. People in many parts of the world have responded to the play's story because they think it resembles or echoes their own.

5. Answers will vary. Sample questions: What caused the sudden rise, and almost equally sudden death, of the Salem witch hunt? In the early 21st century, is it possible that anything similar could ever happen again in America, and if so, why?

## Arthur Miller

### Listening and Viewing, p. 327

Sample answers:

**Segment 1:** Arthur Miller's most famous works are *Death of a Salesman* and *The Crucible*. Students may answer that Arthur Miller wrote about tragic figures, morality, the plight of the common man, and the pressures of society, which were all relevant issues during the time of the Depression.

**Segment 2:** Senator Joseph McCarthy conducted Senate hearings to eliminate alleged communists from American public life. Students may answer that *The Crucible* tells the story of those accused of witchcraft and outcast from society, which can be compared to McCarthy's blacklisting of accused communists in the 1950s.

**Segment 3:** According to Miller, dramas document and respond to history, much like newspapers do, without predicting what will come next. Students may answer that dramas written long ago are still relevant today because their themes and forms can be appealing and meaningful to new audiences.

**Segment 4:** Miller's plays portray power conflicts and social responsibility, and define man in terms of authority and freedom. Students may suggest that Miller was a great social commentator who wrote plays that documented history and are still widely read today.

### Biography: Arthur Miller, p. 328

**1932:** graduated from high school

**1947:** *All My Sons* opened on Broadway

**1949:** won Pulitzer Prize for *Death of a Salesman*

**1953:** wrote *The Crucible*

**1956:** called to testify before the House Committee on Un-American Activities

**1956:** married Marilyn Monroe

### Literary Analysis: Plot and Dramatic Exposition, p. 329

1. Miller reveals information about characters, their backgrounds, and 1690s Salem society.

2. Some of the information is critical to understanding the play, but it would be extremely difficult (if not impossible) to convey through dialogue and traditional stage directions alone.

3. The reader would have to work harder and make more assumptions in order to understand the characters and the setting. Readers might even have to go look up historical information on their own in order to fully appreciate the story.

4. Most students will probably say that the rising action begins when the girls begin shouting out people's names to accuse them of being with the Devil.

5. Most students will probably say that Abigail's desire to protect herself from being exposed as an adulteress and trying to use dark magic to hurt Goody Proctor was the main conflict that started the girls' accusations. Others might say that the general sense of rising fear and the superstitious nature of the community prompted the accusation.

6. Answers will vary. Some might say that learning about Abigail's affair with Proctor is the most important information. Others might say the community's readiness to blame witchcraft for Betty's illness is the most important.

### Reading Strategy: Dialogue and Stage Directions, p. 330

1. Parris believed he was being persecuted wherever he went (background information). As Parris tries to get

information from Abigail, he mentions "enemies" and says they will drive him out if she does not tell him the truth (dialogue). Later, we are told that part of the community had supported a different candidate for Parris's position, but that Parris's supporters prevailed (background information about Thomas Putnam). Several characters are obviously eager to find witchcraft in Parris's house and, therefore, remove him from his post (dialogue).

2. She is an orphan (stage directions) who saw her parents killed by Indians (dialogue). She was a servant to the Proctors, but was dismissed (dialogue).

3. Abigail is "wide-eyed" and "absorbing his presence" when Proctor enters the room (stage directions), implying that she has strong romantic feelings for Proctor. They have been lovers and Abigail wishes they still were (dialogue). Proctor tries to deny any lingering attachment, though (dialogue).

4. Goody Putnam is a "twisted soul of forty-five, a death-ridden woman, haunted by dreams" (stage directions). She has a great deal of grief and pain because seven of her babies have died and she has only one living child (dialogue).

5. She is embarrassed and frightened (stage directions) because she is Proctor's servant (dialogue). She had been told not to leave the house. Now she has been caught at Parris's house disobeying instructions and having a conversation with Abigail that she hopes Proctor did not overhear (dialogue).

## Vocabulary Builder, p. 331

**A.** 1. gratitude—the state of being thankful
2. gratuitous—something that is given to please, rather than in payment

**B.** 1. G; 2. B; 3. E; 4. C; 5. A; 6. D; 7. F

## The Crucible, *Act II,* by Arthur Miller

## Literary Analysis: Allusion, p. 333

### Sample Responses

1. *Cold war* is an allusion to the relationship between the United States and the Soviet Union from the close of World War II to the early 1990s. A cold war is characterized by opposing philosophies and hostility, but lacks open combat.

2. An *Achilles heel* is a weak point in an otherwise strong defense. The mythical warrior Achilles, who could not be harmed because he had been dipped as in infant in the river Styx by his mother, but her hand covered his heel and left it vulnerable. He dies when struck there by an arrow.

3. A *Siren* is an alluring woman, so called because of the seductive nymphs who lured sailors to their doom in Greek and Roman mythology. A *harpy*, also mythical, was a vicious winged monster with the head and trunk of a woman and the tail and talons of a bird of prey.

4. An *ivory tower* is a remote place of contemplation, and the term is often applied to institutions of higher learning, such as universities.

5. According to Greek legend, a sword was suspended by a single hair above the head of courtier Damocles by the king of Syracuse to teach the courtier the perils of a ruler's life. A *sword of Damocles* is any impending danger.

6. In the Bible, God commanded Moses, the leader of the Jews, to part the Red Sea to enable the Jews to escape from the Egyptians into Canaan. So when the crowd opens up to allow Abigail and the other girls through, it is like Moses *parting the Red Sea.*

## Reading Strategy: Make and Confirm Predictions, p. 334

### Sample Responses

1. Prediction: The people accused by the girls will be executed. Background: Many people died during the Salem witch trials. Confirmation: The court has said it will execute any accused person who does not confess to being a witch; some have been sentenced to hang, but none have yet been executed by the end of Act II

2. Prediction: Goody Proctor will be arrested. Background: Abigail is jealous of Goody Proctor and wants her husband. Confirmation: Goody Proctor is arrested before the end of Act II.

3. Prediction: Hale will eventually believe Proctor that Abigail and the others are pretending. Background: Hale is a reasonable and intelligent man who clearly wants to do the right thing. Confirmation: At the end of Act II, Hale still has faith in the court and is hesitant to believe Proctor. So this prediction cannot be confirmed yet. (Hale does come to believe Proctor later in the play.)

4. Prediction: People in Salem will use the witch hysteria to take revenge on their neighbors for past conflicts. Background: Miller states in the background information at the beginning of the play that people would do this. Confirmation: In Act II, Walcott charges Martha Corey with witchcraft because a pig he bought from her died.

5. Prediction: Mary Warren will not testify against the other girls in court. Background: She is terrified and says she cannot. Confirmation: One cannot confirm by the end of Act II whether or not Mary Warren will testify against the other girls. (She does testify against them in Act III.)

## Vocabulary Builder, p. 335

**A.** 1. The root *socio-* refers to society, so *Sociology* is the study of how societies work.
2. The root *onto-* refers to the state of being or existence, so *ontology* is the study or consideration of the nature of being or reality.
3. The root *entomo-* refers to insects, so *entomology* is the study of insects.
4. The root *zoo-* refers to animals, so *zoology* is the study of animals.

**B.** 1. C; 2. B; 3. C; 4. A; 5. C; 6. B

# The Crucible *Act III*, by Arthur Miller

## Literary Analysis: Dramatic and Verbal Irony, p. 337

### Sample Responses

1. The phrase "it melts down all concealment" is ironic because the audience knows that all concealment is not being melted down—Abigail and the girls are "concealing" all sorts of things and apparently getting away with it.

2. Hale asks this question incredulously, and to the audience the *obvious* answer is "yes!" Thus far, every defense *has* been viewed as an attack upon the court.

3. The allusion to the story is ironic because Mary's actions turn out to be the opposite of Tobias's. Instead of freeing someone from the devil, Mary accuses someone of working *with* the devil. Instead of "giving someone sight," Mary "blinds" or fools people by her denial of the truth and her return to Abigail and the girls.

4. Elizabeth's lie is ironic because her husband has insisted that she does not lie. When she does lie, she believes she is saving her husband from the court. In fact, Proctor is condemned by her lie, not for lechery but for being a liar himself.

## Reading Strategy: Evaluate Arguments by Arthur Miller, p. 338

### Sample Responses

1. Danforth argues that people have nothing to fear if they are not witches, but he tells them they will be hanged if they do not confess to being witches once they are accused. This is not logical because they are condemned either way. His evidence is the childrens' testimony and an absence of other witnesses, which is not believable enough.

2. Proctor argues that the girls are lying and none of the accused are in fact witches. His argument is logical because several of the accused can be proven to be good, church-going people who have never done anything bad. His evidence is Mary Warren's confession and his own confession of adultery, which gives Abigail motive; this is believable evidence, but ultimately not enough to convince the judge.

3. Parris argues that Proctor, Corey, and Nurse have come to overthrow the court. His argument is not logical because it is based on his own fear of being exposed and punished if his niece's lie is proven. Parris does not present evidence for his argument, but Cheever reveals that Proctor ripped up the warrant for his wife's arrest and cursed the court, and then Proctor refuses to drop the charge that the girls are lying, even though his wife will be safe until their child is born; these revelations almost convince Danforth that Parris is right.

4. Hale argues that there is sufficient doubt about the girls' truthfulness that the convictions of the accused cannot be upheld. His argument is logical. His evidence is that Mary Warren has confessed, that Proctor would not have revealed his lechery if he were not telling the truth, and that Rebecca is clearly a good woman, which are all believable reasons to cast doubt on the verdicts of the court.

5. Corey argues that Putnam made his daughter accuse a man of witchery in order to get his land. His argument is logical, but he does not have enough evidence to prove it. He says that because only Putnam could afford Jacobs's land, Putnam must have had him accused to get it. He will not give the name of the witness because he wants to protect the man from being punished.

## Vocabulary Builder, p. 339

**A.** 1. Danforth requests that Corey provide an *affidavit*, or formal written statement, of his evidence.

2. Mary Warren's *deposition* was her formal written statement that she and the other girls were pretending all along and never saw townspeople with the Devil.

3. Danforth acted as both the judge and the *prosecutor* when he took the role of a lawyer trying to prove that the girls were telling the truth.

4. Cheever had a *warrant* for Goody Proctor's arrest, which was a document given to him by the court authorizing him to take her into custody.

**B.** 1. B; 2. B; 3. D; 4. C; 5. A; 6. D;

## Literary Analysis: Tragedy and Allegory, p. 341

**A.** 1. John Proctor is the tragic hero because he is involved in a struggle that ends in disaster, is well-respected in the community, and falls due to his pride and honor.

2. Proctor's tragic flaws are that he committed adultery and that he is too proud to confess to a crime he did not commit.

3. Proctor learns that he would rather die with honor by telling the truth than live a lie while others die with the implication of witchcraft attached to their names. If he confesses, he realizes that he makes them all look guilty by association.

**B.** *The Crucible* is an allegory because Miller uses one historical period and setting (seventeenth-century New England) to comment on another (1950s America). The play is an allegory for modern events. The Salem witch trials are an allegory for the anti-Communist hysteria of the 1950s "Red Scare." The comparison is effective because in both cases people could be accused with very little or no proof, and it was extremely difficult to defend oneself against the logical fallacies inherent in the accusations.

## Reading Strategy: Evaluate the Influences of the Historical Period, p. 342

**Sample Responses:**

**Religious:** Puritanism made the people of Salem more likely to believe in the possibility of witchcraft and punish it very harshly.

**Social:** Greed for land, desire to prove their own virtue, jealousy and vengeance were all motives for townspeople to accuse others of being witches.

**Philosophical:** Puritans believed in the value of pure behavior to maintain order in their community and ensure the well-being of all.

**Ethical:** A strong belief in good and evil and the idea that the innocent have nothing to fear drove several of the characters' behavior throughout the play. Other characters based their ethics on logic and basic decency rather than biblical or civic laws.

**Political:** Residents of Salem adhered to strict religion-based laws that were meant to keep public order and protect the souls of the townspeople.

## Vocabulary Builder, p. 343

**A.** 1. *Echo* is a nymph in Greek mythology who pined away for love of Narcissus until only her voice remained.

2. *Volcano* comes from the name of the Roman god Vulcan, the god of fire and metalworking.

3. *Wednesday* is named for Norse god Woden, or Odin.

4. A *museum* is a place for study or art, so named for the Muses of Greek mythology, who inspired writers, artists; and scientists.

**B.** 1. H; 2. E; 3. J; 4. A; 5. F; 6. C; 7. B; 8. I; 9. D; 10. G

## Grammar and Style: Sentence Fragments and Run-Ons, p. 344

**A.** 1. fragment

2. run-on

3. fragment

4. fragment

5. run-on

**B. Sample Corrections:**

1. Reverend Hale tried to get the prisoners to confess.

2. Proctor was not guilty, but he was willing to confess in order to save his life. He wanted to be with his wife and children.

3. Although he spoke his confession willingly, Proctor refused to write it down and sign it.

4. Rebecca Nurse was bravely willing to die rather than confess to being a witch.

5. Proctor changed his mind; he could not write his confession down and lose his honesty.

## The Crucible by Arthur Miller
## *from* Good Night and Good Luck by George Clooney and Grant Heslov

## Comparing Political Drama Past and Present, p. 346

**Reflects the author's political opinion**

*The Crucible* clearly shows that Miller disapproves of the methods of those in charge of the Salem witch trials.

*Good Night and Good Luck* shows how the authors disapprove of McCarthy's methods.

**Characterizes a politician or describes a series of political events**

*The Crucible* describes a series of political events.

*Good Night and Good Luck* characterizes McCarthy by showing what he said and what was said about him.

**Questions inequities and injustices of contemporary society**

By showing how unfair the trials were and how unreliable the witnesses, *The Crucible* exposes the inequities and injustices of the time.

*Good Night and Good Luck* exposes the way McCarthy lied and twisted the truth to make his victims appear guilty of treason.

**Examines a political issue from the past or present or uses past events to comment on current problems**

*The Crucible* examines a political issue from the past, using it to draw parallels to a current problem.

*Good Night and Good Luck* examines a political issue from the present.

## Vocabulary Builder, p. 347

**A.** 1. Sylvia's <u>vulnerability</u> to accusations of incompetence made her an unlikely candidate for president.

2. Because Justin decided to <u>disregard</u> the ringing of his cell phone, he was able to enjoy his vacation.

3. Maureen <u>acknowledges</u> the applause of the audience by taking a bow and then performing an encore.

4. The <u>statute</u> explained the law that the criminal had broken.

**B.** 1. I might help a friend whose vulnerability to food temptations has caused health problems by avoiding fast food places when we are together. _

2. Someone who tended to disregard symptoms of illness might get worse.

3. If a judge acknowledges the validity of certain pieces of evidence, the jury should consider that evidence.

4. The statute regarding dogs and leashes in my neighborhood is that dogs must be on leashes unless they are in their own yards or homes.

# Unit 6

## Names and Terms to Know Worksheet, p. 350

### A. (Possible answers)

1. Ronald Reagan was President of the U.S. from 1981 to 1989.

2. 9/11 refers to September 11, 2001, when terrorist crashed hijacked U.S. airlines into the World Trade Center and Pentagon.

3. Watergate was a scandal that eventually forced President Nixon to resign.

4. Sally Ride was the first female U.S. astronaut.

5. Al Gore was Bill Clinton's Vice President from 1993 to 2001 and lost the controversial 2000 Presidential election to George W. Bush.

6. The U.S. celebrated its Bicentennial—the 200th anniversary of the Declaration of Independence—in 1976.

### B. (Possible responses)

1. People use the Internet to make both casual and business communications, to purchase items of all kind, and to find information, among other things. The Internet is more anonymous than most other forms of person-to-person communication, and makes more information accessible more quickly than any other form of media.

2. Americans were directly confronted with the threat of terrorism in 9/11; there were wars in the Middle East.

3. The Watergate scandal involved political sabotage and other illegal acts and reached up to the White House, forcing President Nixon to resign. In the 2000 election, a long recount of the Florida vote prolonged the decision.

## Essential Question Worksheet, p. 351

### A. (Possible responses)

1. a. People began to communicate all the time through email; they shopped for and purchased items online, sought medical advice, and so on. They used the Internet to find information to both casual and important questions.

   b. Historians have begun to regard the contributions of minority populations not as marginal but as part of mainstream American culture.

   c. Americans came together in the wake of the tragedy. They became much more concerned about security at all times.

2. a. Computers made it easy to share personal expressions with large groups of people and organizations. Because the communication is not face to face, the communicator is essentially anonymous and can hide or change his or her onscreen identity.

   b. Rather than encouraging different groups to lose their differences in the "melting pot," the nation has begun to celebrate individual cultures for themselves and preserve rather than eliminate diversity.

3. a. Mainstream American literature included works by men and women who were African Americans, American Indians, Latinos, and Asian Americans.

   b. Computer technology makes it easy for a work of literature to be circulated online to millions. In addition, readers can purchased printed works over the Internet. In some cases, writers produce interactive works, in which readers participate in shaping the work.

   c. Americans explored the themes of personal and cultural identity, the changing nature of family, the blending of truth and illusion, and the meaning and impact of success.

### B. (Possible responses)

1. Diversity would suggest many choices on a menu, since it refers to differences.

2. A commercial view of a product would focus on how to market and sell it.

3. I get most of my news from the Internet.

## Essential Question Worksheet, p. 352

### A. (Possible responses)

1. a. Tyler, Russo, Ford, Jones, and Proux are among the writers who explore recognizable cities and towns and other areas of everyday American life.

   b. Philip Roth re-imagined recent American history transformed by prejudice; Cormac McCarthy re-imagined America in a post-apocalyptic state.

2. a. American literature explores environmental problems such as pollution and ecoterrorism.

   b. Nonfiction writers Dillard and McPhee and poets Snyder, Merwin, and Ammons focus on the natural world.

3. a. Characters now use up-to-date technology—cellphones and computers—to communicate with each other. Readers and authors can communicate directly with one another over the Internet.

   b. television, movies, and music

   c. Cyberliterature is literature that takes advantage of the capabilities of the computer to make texts more fluid and include actual sounds and images to text.

### B. (possible responses)

1. It would be futuristic because cyberspace refers to the virtual world of computers.

2. Local property taxes would not be a global concern.

3. I would add a second story to my house.

## Essential Question Workshop p. 353

### A. (Possible responses)

1. a. America is a highly diverse society, accentuating the differences of individual groups, and literature reflects that quality.

b. The popular and literary have merged, as have fiction and nonfiction.

2. a. It means that the author makes the reader aware of the artificial nature of the work.

   b. The horrors of the twentieth century made it impossible to assume that the world itself made sense, and so literature was not expected to make sense of it either.

   c. Literature today regards the past as capable of being revised, at least in art.

3. a. Toni Morrison, Andrea Barrett, and Dave Eggers

   b. Louise Gluck, Ann Lauterbach, Yusef Komunyakaa, and Li-Young Lee

### B. (Possible responses)

1. The poet might write a play or novel.
2. global positioning systems
3. Self-conscious persons are likely to be nervous, because they are always thinking about how others view them.

## Follow-Through Activities, p. 354

### A. Check Your Comprehension

Guidelines: Students should complete the chart with other concepts appropriate to the period and the groups that are associated with these concepts.

### B. Extend Your Learning

Guidelines: Students should complete the chart with answers that will help them to do their research.

## *from* the Author's Desk

## Julie Alvarez Introduces "Antojos" p. 355

### Suggested Answers

1. It became the first chapter of Alvarez's novel *How the García Girls Lost Their Accents.*

2. As an immigrant who was not a native English speaker, she wanted to start small in the literature of her adoptive country.

3. It made her treat prose as if it were poetry, something beautifully and carefully crafted in which each word is carefully chosen to be as precise as possible.

4. In his biography she read that Wolfe wrote a novel called *You Can't Go Home Again,* an idea she explores in her story.

5. It is based on Julia Alvarez and her experiences of returning home to her native Dominican Republic to visit relatives there.

6. It shows that you can go home again in some ways but not in others.

7. An essay directly addresses an idea, supporting it with facts and examples, while a story like "Antojos" shows characters and events that convey the idea as a life experience.

8. She included it as part of the realistic setting details of her story. It came to be seen as a symbol.

## Julia Alvarez

## Listening and Viewing, p. 356

### Suggested Answers

### Segment 1: Meet Julia Alvarez

- She spent her childhood as part of a large, extended family in the Dominican Republican.

- Some classmates were unfriendly and made fun of her accent, but a wonderful teacher taught her to love reading, which helped connect her to the culture.

### Segment 2: Julia Alvarez on the Short Story

- It should start with action that gets the reader involved.

- It should end as close to the middle as possible.

### Segment 3: Julia Alvarez on the Writing Process

- To be a writer, you must develop the habit of avoiding distractions and writing every day whether you feel like it or not.

- Stories do not work that way; the writer tries different things, and characters sometimes take the writer in unexpected directions. However, the writer must also be willing to edit out material that takes away from the story.

### Segment 4: Julia Alvarez on the Rewards of Writing

- They do not play a role; she writes because she does not know how to live without writing.

- It helps her to make meaning of life and find the true pattern of life. It also gives her deep pleasure because writing is her calling and her passion.

## "Antojos" by Julia Alvarez

## Literary Analysis: Plot Structure, p. 357

### Possible Responses

In medias res: "Once her own engine was off, she heard the sound of another motor, approaching, a pained roar as if the engine were falling apart"; the story begins with Yolanda in the middle of her car trip without explaining why she is traveling or where she is traveling to; this technique piques readers' interest by making us wonder who this woman is, why she is traveling, and where she is going.

Flashback: "In the capital, her aunts had plied her with what she most craved after so many years away. 'Any little antojo, you must tell us!'"; the story flashes back to a time before her car trip, when she had first arrived on the island

and was visiting her aunts; this flashback tells us that the aunts are wealthy women who can provide her with anything she desires—any *antojo*.

Foreshadowing: "It was a little cluster of houses on either side of the road, a good place to stretch her legs before what she'd heard was a steep and slightly [her aunts had warned her 'very'] dangerous descent to the coast"; the sentence foreshadows difficulties or dangers—real or imagined—that Yolanda will face on her car trip; the passage encourages the reader to anticipate that Yolanda will have some kind of problem on her car trip, perhaps even a dangerous one—it thus anticipates the flat tire and her encounter with the men with the machetes. even though the danger they pose to her is only in her own mind.

## Reading Strategy: Make Predictions, p. 358
### Possible Responses
1. The "hunger march" shows that there are many poor people in the Dominican Republic, so Yolanda will probably encounter signs of poverty on her trip.
2. This hint about the gulf between rich and poor in the Dominican Republic indicates that Yolanda will probably see signs of his disparity on her trip.
3. Yolanda will take off on some kind of trip or detour involving the satisfaction of her yearning for guavas.
4. Yolanda will encounter some sort of danger—real or imagined—from the desperate poor people on the road as she travels by car.
5. The young boy will have some sort of problem or bad encounter with rich people.
6. Yolanda will have some sort of problem with the car as she makes her detour in search of guavas.

## Vocabulary Builder, p. 359
**A.** 1. netting or canvas hung from ropes at both ends and used as a bed; from the Spanish word *hamaca*.
2. public square of marketplace, an open area; shopping center; taken directly from Spanish
3. courtyard or inner, open area of a building; paved area near a house, used for outdoor sitting or eating; taken directly from Spanish
4. powder made from cacao seeds; crushed chocolate; a drink made with milk or hot water and powdered chocolate; from the Spanish word *cacao*.

**B.** 1. C; 2. D; 3. C; 4. B; 5. C

## "Everyday Use" by Alice Walker

## Literary Analysis: Characterization, p. 361
### Sample Answers
Possible responses might include the following: Standard English: "Sometimes I dream a dream in which Dee and I are suddenly brought together on a TV program of this sort. Out of a dark and soft-seated limousine I am ushered into a bright room filled with many people." What it reveals about

narrator's character: She is an imaginative woman and longs to be reconciled with her daughter Dee.

Dialect: " 'Why don't you take one or two of the others?' I asked. 'These old things was just done by me and Big Dee from some tops your grandma pieced before she died.'" What it reveals about narrator's character: She is a skilled craftsperson with a deep feeling for her family and its traditions.

## Reading Strategy: Contrast Characters, p. 362
### Sample Responses
1. His mouth is twisted into a frown; his teeth like dirty jagged stones.
2. She gently sliced an apple on the smooth, clean counter.
3. She marched into the living room, her hands waving in the air.
4. She gently lifted the lid and peeked inside to see if the quilts were there.
5. She gazed silently at the simmering stew.

## Vocabulary Builder, p. 363
**A.** 1. doctorate; 2. documented; 3. docent; 4. doctrinaire
**B.** 1. C; 2. B; 3. D; 4. B

## Grammar and Style: Transitional Expressions, p. 364
**A.** Sample Response
1. between the eyes [spatial relationship]
2. before we raised the money [time relationship]
3. as she walks closer [time relationship]
4. down the road [spatial relationship]
5. where hands pushing the dasher up and down [spatial relationship]
6. like those lavender ones [comparison]

**B.** Sample Response

Paragraphs must use transitions and transitional phrases.

## "Everything Stuck to Him" by Raymond Carver

## Literary Analysis: Author's Style, p. 366
### Sample Answer
Possible responses: No quotation marks in dialogue—adds to bare-bones feel of the story, and allows dialogue to blend in with the action; no names given to father and daughter—encourages the reader to focus on their inner thoughts and feelings rather than external details of their lives; The husband and wife are called "boy" and "girl"—the names "boy" and "girl" emphasize the youth of the husband and wife and encourage the reader to regard them as standing in for all young couples of this type; No physical descriptions of characters—encourages readers to focus on inner thoughts and feelings rather than external features; Simple, direct language—encourages reader to focus on details of story and character instead of abstract ideas.

## Reading Strategy: Ask Questions, p. 367

**Sample Responses**

1. The two characters are the father and his daughter. The main clue is that he says, "I could tell you about something that happened when you were a baby."

2. The omniscient narrator (the author) narrates the outer story. The father narrates the inner story.

3. This admission of interest in girl's sisters shows that boy has a roving eye that might create problems for their marriage in the future.

4. "Boy" and "girl" are no longer together. "Girl" is not there in Milan, and there is no mention of her in the present—only in the story from twenty years earlier.

5. On a surface level, the title refers to the breakfast that sticks to his long johns after he spills the meal in his lap. On a deeper level, it might refer to the way the emotions of that period of his life seem to stick as to him so many years later as he retells the "inner" story.

## Vocabulary Builder, p. 368

**A.** 1. No, he was often not free of exam pressures on his birthday, because *coincide* means "to occupy the same place in space or in time."

2. No, Juanita does not lack goals if she is known for her ambitions, because *ambitions* means "desires to achieve particular ends."

3. Yes, people would be likely to notice the decor of the hotel lobby, because *striking* means "attracting attention through unusual or conspicuous qualities."

4. No, he would not have slept soundly through the night, because *fitfully* means "erratically or intermittently."

**B.** 1. D; 2. B; 3. C; 4. B

---

## "Traveling Through the Dark" by William Stafford
## "The Secret" by Denise Levertov
## "The Gift" by Li-Young Lee

## Literary Analysis: Epiphany, p. 370

**Sample Answer**

1. This is not a true epiphany; although the speaker does make a discovery, it has not yet provoked any larger insight into himself or life.

2. This is a true epiphany; the speaker reaches the major insight that preserving the safety of the people in the oncoming cars in more important than trying to preserve the life of the fawn inside the lifeless doe.

3. This is a true epiphany—there can be no insight or truth more important or profound than discovering the secret of life.

4. Students might suggest that this is a true epiphany as well, for the speaker finds inspiration in the girls' passion and idealism about discovering the secret of life; the speaker acknowledges, thanks to the girls' example, that there may be such a secret after all.

5. This is not a true epiphany—it describes a moment that led to an epiphany for the speaker, but it is only a description of an event, not a description of a profound or sudden insight.

6. This is a true epiphany. The passage describes how the father's care in removing the metal shard inspired the boy to understand the importance of love and compassion, prompting him to return his father's love with a kiss.

## Reading Strategy: Interpret Poetry, p. 371

**Sample Responses**

1. Students might note that the speaker of these lines is the poet herself. She is commenting on the enthusiastic reaction to her poems by two young girls that she has never met in person. The lines show that the poem is about how the poet gets as much inspiration from her readers' reactions to her ideas as from the ideas themselves. It even shows that the readers' reactions can help the poet to find meanings in her poems that she didn't even know were there.

2. Students might note that the title "Traveling Through the Dark" has a double meaning. In the literal sense, it refers to the speaker driving at nighttime on a lonely country road. On a deeper level, it refers to an emotional and ethical darkness—the speaker's inability to find a clear answer to the dilemma of whether to toss aside the carcass of the doe even though there is a living fawn in it. His decision to toss the carcass does not dispel the element of ambiguity and doubt that lingers over this agonizing decision.

3. Students might suggest the gift in "The Gift" is the gift of love that the father gives to his son in the example of the care and compassion he shows in removing a metal splinter from his hand when he was a terrified little boy, thinking he would die. The image of "silver tear" relates to the emotion the boy feels at his father's tenderness, and the "tiny flame" is a kind of enduring warmth that the father has ignited in his soul, a warmth that he carries over to his wife when he performs a similar procedure on her with the same love and compassion.

## Vocabulary Builder, p. 372

**A.** 1. exhaustible; 2. exhausted; 3. exhaustively
**B.** 1. C; 2. B; 3. D

## Literary Analysis: Voice, p. 374

**Sample Responses**

"Who Burns for the Perfection of Paper": The tone of this poem is reflective. The poet recalls the agonizing labor he endured manufacturing legal pads as a youth. He provides images of the glue, "hands oozing," and "palms burned." He now reflects upon and connects these images to the perfectly bound legal pads he later used at law school ("every open lawbook was a pair of hands upturned and burning").

**"Camouflaging the Chimera":** This poem about guerilla warfare in Vietnam expresses a tone of intense, watchful waiting, at first through the use of concrete details ("We hugged bamboo & leaned / against a breeze against the river"); but it also builds to a tone of desperation and anguish by scattering surreal images among the matter-of-fact ones ("slow-dragging with the ghosts," "we waited till the moon touched metal," "black silk wrestling iron through grass," "a world revolved / under each man's eyelid").

**"Streets":** The tone of this poem is dreamlike and meditative, with the poet stretching words through figures of speech to try to grapple with the mystery of death ("the streets he lived on / grow a little shorter," "the sky which sews and sews, tirelessly sewing, / drops her purple hem." The voice is gentle and mystical, gazing both ways from the border between life and death ("They dream thickly, / dream double, they wake from a dream / into another one. . . .)

## Reading Strategy: Analyze Author's Implicit Beliefs, p. 375

### Sample Responses

Possible responses: **"Who Burns for the Perfection of Paper"**—Author's beliefs: behind many manufactured products is a process of factory labor that is harsh and demeaning to the humans who make them. Details: "the glue would sting, / hands oozing / till both palms burned / at the punchclock"; "a pair of hands / upturned and burning." **"Camouflaging the Chimera"**—Author's beliefs: war takes an almost inhuman toll of anxiety and fear on soldiers of both sides. Details: "something almost broke inside us. . .."; "we held our breath, ready to spring the L-shaped / ambush . . ." **"Streets":** The death of a human being diminishes the world around him/her; in death we cross over from one kind of dream into another. Details: "A man leaves the world / and the streets he lived on / grow a little shorter"; "They dream thickly, / dream, double, they wake from a dream / into another one. . . ."

## Vocabulary Builder, p. 376

**A.** 1. terrain
2. crevices
3. refuge
4. terrain
5. refuge
6. crevices

**B.** 1. in the air
2. yes
3. yes

**C.** 1. C; 2. A; 3. C

## "Halley's Comet" by Stanley Kunitz

## Literary Analysis: Free Verse, p. 378

### Sample Response

Examples of each kind of ending might include the following: End-stopped lines: "there'd be no school tomorrow. / A

red-bearded preacher . . ."—emphasizes break between idea of no school and presence of the preacher; "with my mother and sisters; / but I felt excited too . . ."—emphasizes contrast between his anxiety and his excitement; Enjambed Lines: "wrote its name in chalk / across the board and told use / it was roaring . . ."—emphasizes continuity of process of writing on the board and speaking at the same time; "They never heard me steal / into the stairwell hall and climb / the ladder to the fresh night air"; emphasizes the secretiveness of "stealing" into the stairwell and the continuous action of climbing the ladder.

## Reading Strategy: Identify Changes in Tense and Tone, p. 379

### Sample Response

Possible response: Type of Change: Change in tense and tone. Where It Occurs: "So mother scolded me / and sent me early to my room. / The whole family's asleep /except for me"; Possible Meaning: past tense in first two lines, present tense in last two lines emphasizes shift in recounting mealtime events to the speaker's current urgent excitement that keeps him awake. Type of Change: Change in tense and tone. Where It Occurs: between end of first stanza and beginning of second stanza. Possible meaning: emphasizes break between memory of past events and the more immediate and pressing sense of the boy praying to / addressing his dead father in the hopes that the end of the world will reunite them.

## Vocabulary Builder, p. 380

**A.** 1. No, he was not saying it in a whisper, because *proclaiming* means "declaring proudly or openly."

2. Yes, he was passing judgment on the sinners, because *repent* means "feel sorry" or "feel regret," so he was implying that their sins were wrong and required them to make amends or seek forgiveness.

3. No, the narrator did not tell his mother and sister, because *steal* means "sneak"; he went to the roof without wanting them to know about it.

**B.** 1. B; 2. C; 3. A

## "The Latin Deli: An Ars Poetica"
### by Judith Ortiz Cofer

## Literary Analysis: Imagery, p. 382

### Sample Response

Students might cite some of the following: dried codfish, green plantains (smell, sight, touch)—foods associated with native countries; Bustelo coffee (smell, sight)—brand associated with Latin subculture; Patroness of Exiles (sight)—contributes to sense of deli as sacred gathering ground for Latinos; plain wide face, ample bosom (sight)—evokes image of deli owner as maternal figure who brings community together; plain ham and cheese (sight, smell, touch, taste)—an item that is familiar and comforting to Latinos immigrants from diverse lands; fragile old man lost in the folds of his winter coat (sight, touch)—reinforces idea of Latinos as lost in alien culture of North America.

## Reading: Analyzing Sensory Details, p. 383
### Sample Response
Students' responses might include the following sensory details from the poem: "heady mix of smells from the open bins / of dried codfish, the green plantains . . .," "selling canned memories," "a pound of Bustelo coffee," "her plain wide face, her ample bosom / resting on her plump arms . . .," "the stale candy of everyone's childhood . . . ," "plain ham and cheese," "the fragile old man lost in the folds / of his winter coat." What the details have in common: they evoke the sensory experience of the customers' homelands, a kind of home away from home for the Latinos in exile in a North American city. Overall feeling or idea expressed by details: the importance of feeling a sense of home or belonging, especially when the surrounding culture is different from one's familiar traditions and values.

## Vocabulary Builder, p. 384
**A.** 1. False; a heady mix of smells would be intoxicating and therefore very noticeable.
2. False; if you had ample supplies, you would have enough, so there would be no need to go out shopping.
3. True; experiencing a number of disillusions means you would be exposed to truths about life and therefore have fewer false notions.
4. True; if you had mastered all the material for the test, there would be no need to divine, or guess, the answers, because you would know them.

**B.** 1. D; 2. A; 3. A; 4. C

## "Onomatopoeia" by William Safire

## Literary Analysis: Expository Essay, p. 386
### Sample Responses
**A.** Students' responses might include the following: "six copy editors will get zapped"—formal English: six copy editors will be dismissed from their jobs; "started us all yakking toward language"—started us all progressing toward spoken language; "Edgar Allan Poe one-upped him"—Edgar Allan Poe outdid him; "in the crunch"—in a quandary or difficult situation; "has blasted its way into the dictionaries"—"has become listed formally in the dictionaries."

**B.** Students essays should be brief, using at least two idiomatic words or phrases to establish an informal and/or humorous tone.

## Reading Strategy: Paraphrase, p. 387
### Sample Responses
**A.** Possible responses: 1. Some people hold the *bow-wow theory*, according to which language originated from people imitating sounds from nature and animals. 2. People create new words by imitating sounds that people hear only in their imagination. 3. That use filled a need for a new usage and expanded the vocabulary.

**B.** Sample response: Onomatopoeia means "words that imitate a sound." Some people think that spoken language originated in this way—people imitating sounds of animals or nature. Onomatopoeia can imitate imaginary as well as real sounds—*zap* in an example.

## Vocabulary Builder, p. 388
### Possible Responses
**A.** 1. No, she is asking for a word that is similar in meaning to *stubborn*, because *synonymous* means "alike in meaning or significance."
2. Yes, Safire is discussing the origin of the word *onomatopoeia*, because one can derive—or trace the meaning of—*onomatopoeia* from the earlier Greek word.
3. No, the theory is not well grounded in facts because *speculation* means "taking to be true on the basis of insufficient evidence."
4. Yes, he is talking about the way the word came into being, because *coinage* in this context means "something made up or invented."

**B.** 1. D; 2. A; 3. A; 4. C

## "Coyote v. Acme" by Ian Frazier

## Literary Analysis: Parody, p. 390
### Sample Responses
1. It is ridiculous that an animal—even a cartoon-character animal—would be launching a lawsuit. It is also ridiculous and amusing to think that a coyote, who roams in the wild, would be considered a legal "resident" of one or more states. It is also amusing that the brief refers to an animal as "Mr. Coyote."
2. It is both ridiculous and exaggerated to think of a predator's natural hunting activities as "making a living." It is also a form of humorous exaggeration to think of a wild predator as "self-employed."
3. Part of the ridiculous and exaggerated element here is the overblown legal language—"sudden and precipitate force"; the absurd exaggeration of Coyote's forelimbs stretching to fifty feet adds to the humor.
4. The ridiculous, exaggerated extent of the injuries here has a comical effect because such a disastrous combination of injuries would be unimaginable in real life.
5. This exaggerated list of damages is amusing because it parodies the wildly inflated dollar claims that are typical of many lawsuits; it is also amusing in the exaggerated details of kinds of damages claimed, including "days lost from professional occupation," as though a coyote's stalking and hunting of a bird can be considered a "professional occupation."

## Reading Strategy: Cause and Effect, p. 391

### Sample Responses

| Example | Key Word or Phrase | Cause(s) | Effect(s) |
|---|---|---|---|
| 1. "Mr. Coyote is self-employed and thus not eligible for Workmen's compensation." | thus | Coyote is self-employed. | He is not eligible for workmen's compensation. |
| 2. "Mr. Coyote vigorously attempted to follow this maneuver but was unable to, due to poorly designed steering system on the Rocket Sled and a faulty or nonexistent braking system." | due to | poorly designed steering system, faulty or nonexistent braking system | Coyote was unable to follow the specified maneuver. |
| 3. "The force of this impact then caused the springs to rebound, whereupon Mr. Coyote was thrust skyward." | caused | force of impact | Springs rebounded, Coyote was thrust skyward. |
| 4. The sequence of collisions resulted in systemic physical damage to Mr. Coyote, viz., flattening of the cranium, sideways displacement of the tongue. . . . | resulted in | sequence of collisions | Physical damage to Coyote, including flattening of the cranium and sideways displacement of the tongue. |

## Vocabulary Builder, p. 392

### Possible Responses

**A.** 1. C; 2. A; 3. A;

**B.** 1. B; 2. D; 3. C; 4. D 5. A; 6. C

### "Urban Renewal" by Sean Ramsay

### "Playing for the Fighting Sixty-Ninth" by William Harvey

## Primary Sources: Oral History and E-mail, p. 394

1. Students might suggest that Ramsay was trying to come to terms with his feelings of shock and grief by seeking out the tokens of other people's feelings and reactions to the tragic events of 9-11.
2. New Yorkers had become far more compassionate and considerate than usual, as exemplified in the sanitation workers' concern to protect the impromptu memorials from the rain and put them back out the next day.
3. It tell about events in intimate, familiar language, expresses spontaneous thoughts and feelings, and provides moving details, all of which ar often absent from news reports.
4. Harvey's account shows that in emergencies people can tap wells of energy, stamina, and dedication that would not be available to them under normal circumstances.
5. The written e-mail can allow the author to provide much more detail and more thoughtful reflection on events than one would typically find in a spontaneous oral account like "Urban Renewal."

## Vocabulary Builder p. 395

**A.** 1. A; 2. C; 3. D; 4. B 5. D; 6. C; 7. B; 8. D 9. A; 10. C

### "One Day, Broken in Two" by Anna Quindlen

## Literary Analysis: Comparison and Contrast Essay, p. 396

### Sample Response

Possible responses: Personal Feelings—secure, confident / insecure, wary; Daily Routines—as usual / as usual, with added attention to family and personal ties; Travel—normal / gradually returning to normal; What Kind of People Are We—mostly proud of our achievements and culture / doubting the worth of some aspects of our achievements and culture; What Kind of World Do We Live In—ordered, comprehensible / frightening, confusing."

## Reading Strategy: Relate a Literary Work to Primary Source Documents, p. 397

**Possible Responses**

| Primary Source | Where It to Find It | Advantage of Source |
|---|---|---|
| Newspaper article | Library microfilm, Internet | University and government archives, Internet |
| Video footage | Internet, TV stations | Gives immediate audiovisual impact of events |
| Personal eyewitness accounts | Internet, personal interviews, newspaper and magazine interviews and reporting, essays, articles | Tells what it was like to be in the middle of the events |
| Government communications and activities | Government archives | Explains how government officials and first responders reacted to and handled events |
| Reports of scientists and engineers who inspected and analyzed the evidence at the scene | University and government archives, Internet | Helps to understand the physical chain of cause-and-effect of the events of 9-11. |

## Vocabulary Builder, p. 398

**Possible Responses**

**A.** 1. mundane
2. revelations
3. savagery
4. prosperity
5. induce

**B.** 1. B; 2. A; 3. C; 4. A 5. D

## "For the Love of Books" by Rita Dove
## "Mother Tongue" by Amy Ian

## Literary Analysis: Reflective Essay, p. 400

**Sample Responses**

1. She describes having to make corn tortillas although she does not know how. This makes her recall having to write a critical essay for her MFA.
2. These experiences made her feel anxious, trapped "like the woman in the fairy tale who was locked in a room and ordered to spin straw into gold."
3. These stories reveal that Cisneros is strong-willed, has confidence in herself, and has learned to trust her intuition and ability.

4. Dove realized that writers are real people, not just names on title pages or dust jackets.
5. Her reading tastes reveal that she values literature in its many forms.
6. They reveal that Dove was a shy and introverted child who found comfort in books and valued them for the boundless possibilities they represented.
7. The answers to math questions were precise and objective, whereas the answers to the English questions seemed to be a matter of opinion and personal experience.
8. In her adolescence, Tan was embarrassed by her mother's imperfect English; as an adult, she saw it as a part of her mother's unique way of expressing her thoughts and feelings.

## Reading Strategy: Outlining, p. 401

**Sample Responses**
### "For the Love of Books"
Main Idea: "I have always been passionate about books." Supporting Details: "warm heft in may hand"; "the warm spot caused by their intimate weight in my lap"; "I loved the crisp whisper of a page turning, the musky odor of old paper"; "leather bindings sent me into an ecstasy."

### "Mother Tongue"
Main Idea: People in the United States who do not speak perfect standard English are treated with less dignity than those with a better command of English.

Supporting Details: Tan's mother has trouble getting desired results from her stockbroker; her mother is dismissed rudely by the hospital workers who have lost the film of her CAT scan.

## Grammar and Style: Parallel Structure, p. 402

**Sample Responses**

**A.** "For the Love of Books": "My idea of a bargain was to <u>go</u> to the public library, <u>wander</u> along the bookshelves, and <u>emerge</u> with a chin-high stack of books. . . ."; ". . . she <u>asked</u> my parents instead, <u>signed</u> me and a classmate out of school one day, and <u>took</u> us to meet a writer."

"Mother Tongue": "That was the language that helped shape the way I <u>saw things</u>, <u>expressed things</u>, <u>made sense</u> of the world"; ". . . people in department stores, at banks, and at restaurants <u>did not</u> take her seriously, <u>did not</u> give her good service. . . ."

**B.** 1. Tan's mother is shown getting rebuffed and enduring rude behavior.
2. The writer hopes to achieve a sense of truth and to reach a receptive audience.
3. Amy Tan is recognized for seeing a world in which various cultures are of equal value and for astutely portraying of family relationships.

## Vocabulary Builder, p. 403

**Sample Responses**

1. The jeweler charged Tina an additional fee to *inscribe* the ring with her name.
2. The original *manuscript* of the novel is on display at the museum.

**B.** 1. B; 2. A; 3. D; 4. C; 5. C;

## *from* The Woman Warrior by Maxine Hong Kingston
## *from* The Names by N. Scott Momaday

## Literary Analysis: Memoirs, p. 405

**Sample Responses**

1. The narrative point of view is the first person. This point of view is typical of most memoirs because the author is usually talking about incidents that he or she has directly experienced.
2. Students' responses might include some of the following: Event: receiving a horse as a gift from his parents; Significance: riding the horse allows him to see the world from a different, more independent perspective. Experience: Taking a long journey on his horse; Significance: Seeing new sights and meeting new people spurs his emotional and intellectual growth ("My mind soared"). Experience: Training his horse to race; Significance: It teaches him the value of discipline, teamwork, and working toward a goal.
3. The piece focuses on Brave Orchid's personal impressions. Students might note that passage in which Brave Orchid describes the habits of her American children or the passage in which she describes the young soldiers.
4. *The Woman Warrior* is different from other memoirs in that it is written in the third person and it is based on Kingston's mother and the "talk stories" Kingston heard as a child.

## Reading Strategy: Relate to Your Own Experiences, p. 406

**Sample Responses**

1. The woman warrior in the title refers to one of the writer's ancestors in China—a brave heroine of one of her mother's "talk stories." The title might also refer to

every Chinese and Chinese American woman in the book, including Brave Orchid, Moon Orchid, and their daughters.
2. Ellis Island is in the harbor off New York City. Brave Orchid and her husband went to Ellis Island when they first immigrated to the United States.
3. China was war-torn, and she wanted to join her husband in New York.
4. Students might mention any of a number of minor superstitions they have or have observed in others: counting, not walking under ladders, sitting in a certain chair while rooting for the home team, and so on.
5. Students might mention parents' disapproval of things like fast food, certain kinds of music, hair and clothing styles, and so on.
6. Students should describe any prolonged or anxious experience waiting for someone, whether in a public or private environment.

## Vocabulary Builder, p. 407

**A.** 1. audiovisual
    2. audiology
    3. audience
    4. audible
**B.** 1. D; 2. C; 3. A; 4. B; 5. C

## Grammar and Style: Creating Sentence Variety, p. 408

**Sample Answers**

1. The first, complex, sentence gives Kingston plenty of room in which to set the overall scene. The second, simple, sentence conveys the most important information with the added punch of brevity.
2. The first, compound, sentence allows Kingston to pose the various alternatives. The second, complex, sentence allows her to express Brave Orchid's anxious feelings about her son.
3. The first, complex, sentence allows Momaday to set the scene of the riding adventure. The shorter simple sentence that follows literally picks up the pace, as the content of the sentence indicates.

# Standardized Test Practice

## Screening Test, p. 411

| | | | |
|---|---|---|---|
| 1. C | 7. A | 13. A | 19. C |
| 2. H | 8. F | 14. H | 20. J |
| 3. A | 9. A | 15. A | 21. B |
| 4. J | 10. J | 16. H | 22. F |
| 5. C | 11. A | 17. C | 23. C |
| 6. G | 12. J | 18. F | 24. G |

## Practice Test 1, p. 417

| | |
|---|---|
| 1. D | 16. D |
| 2. A | 17. D |
| 3. C | 18. C |
| 4. B | 19. B |
| 5. C | 20. D |
| 6. D | 21. D |
| 7. B | 22. D |
| 8. C | 23. A |
| 9. D | 24. B |
| 10. D | 25. D |
| 11. D | 26. A |
| 12. D | 27. C |
| 13. C | 28. A |
| 14. A | 29. B |
| 15. B | 30. D |

## Practice Test 2, p. 424

| | |
|---|---|
| 1. B | 16. A |
| 2. C | 17. A |
| 3. D | 18. C |
| 4. A | 19. B |
| 5. C | 20. C |
| 6. D | 21. D |
| 7. B | 22. D |
| 8. C | 23. B |
| 9. A | 24. C |
| 10. D | 25. B |
| 11. B | 26. C |
| 12. D | 27. B |
| 13. C | |
| 14. C | |
| 15. D | |

# SAT/ACT Practice Test, p. 429

## CRITICAL READING

### Section 1: Sentence Completion

| | | |
|---|---|---|
| 1. D | 6. D | 11. B |
| 2. A | 7. A | 12. A |
| 3. A | 8. B | 13. C |
| 4. C | 9. D | |
| 5. D | 10. E | |

### Section 2: Reading Comprehension

| | | |
|---|---|---|
| 14. D | 25. A | 36. A |
| 15. E | 26. C | 37. E |
| 16. A | 27. B | 38. A |
| 17. D | 28. C | 39. C |
| 18. A | 29. E | 40. C |
| 19. C | 30. A | 41. A |
| 20. D | 31. E | 42. D |
| 21. B | 32. C | 43. A |
| 22. E | 33. B | 44. B |
| 23. B | 34. A | |
| 24. D | 35. B | |

## WRITING

| | | |
|---|---|---|
| 45. B | 57. C | 69. D |
| 46. C | 58. C | 70. A |
| 47. D | 59. E | 71. B |
| 48. B | 60. B | 72. C |
| 49. B | 61. B | 73. C |
| 50. E | 62. E | 74. A |
| 51. D | 63. D | 75. D |
| 52. C | 64. C | 76. B |
| 53. B | 65. D | 77. E |
| 54. A | 66. E | 78. B |
| 55. D | 67. A | 79. C |
| 56. A | 68. A | |

Each student's response should feature a clear central idea, strong organization, vivid and appropriate language, and correct use of grammar and mechanics.